THE FAMILY CHEF

THE FAMILY CHEF

by Jewels and Jill Elmore

with Ann Marsh

PHOTOGRAPHY BY PETRINA TINSLAY

A CELEBRA BOOK

Celebra
Published by New American Library, a division of Penguin Group (USA) Inc., 375 Hudson Street, New
York, New York 10014, USA • Penguin Group (Canada), 90 Eglinton Avenue East, Suite 700, Toronto,
Ontario M4P 2Y3, Canada (a division of Pearson Penguin Canada Inc.) • Penguin Books Ltd., 80 Strand,
London WC2R 0RL, England • Penguin Ireland, 25 St. Stephen's Green, Dublin 2, Ireland (a division
of Penguin Books Ltd.) • Penguin Group (Australia), 250 Camberwell Road, Camberwell, Victoria
3124, Australia (a division of Pearson Australia Group Pty. Ltd.) • Penguin Books India Pvt. Ltd., 11
Community Centre, Panchsheel Park, New Delhi - 110 017, India • Penguin Group (NZ), 67 Apollo
Drive, Rosedale, North Shore 0632, New Zealand (a division of Pearson New Zealand Ltd.) • Penguin
Books (South Africa) (Pty.) Ltd., 24 Sturdee Avenue, Rosebank, Johannesburg 2196, South Africa

Penguin Books Ltd., Registered Offices: 80 Strand, London WC2R 0RL, England

Published by Celebra, an imprint of New American Library,
a division of Penguin Group (USA) Inc.

First Printing, May 2009
10 9 8 7 6 5 4 3

LIBRARY OF CONGRESS CATALOGING-IN-PUBLICATION DATA:

Elmore, Jewels.
   The family chef/Jewels and Jill Elmore, with Ann Marsh; photography by
Petrina Tinslay.
      p. cm.
   Includes bibliographical references and index.
   ISBN 978-0-451-22641-9
   1. Cookery.   2. Cookery (Natural foods)   I. Elmore, Jill.   II. Marsh, Ann.   III. Title.

   TX714.E453 2009
   641.5-dc22   2008050727

Set in Din
Designed by Pauline Neuwirth, Neuwirth & Associates, Inc.

This book is dedicated to Nana and Papa,
who taught us by example how to work hard
and with pride, but more importantly to do it
with love and gratitude.
Sal and Ginny . . . we miss you every day.

contents

foreword

THE CULINARILY CHALLENGED period of my life, which I like to refer to as "B.J.: Before Jewels," wasn't pretty, people!

At best it was prepackaged Zone meals, overcooked takeout and scrounging for the occasional piece of cheese. And I was making a decent living, so what was my excuse for low energy?

Until the secret of how important it is to nourish oneself is introduced into your life, you live in the dark and at the mercy of processed foods.

I used to think anything packaged as "low-fat" was good for me; I was an avid consumer of artificial sugar and butter substitutes—I was living amongst all the impressionists.

Then Saucy, Inspired and Graceful—otherwise known as Jewels—walked into my kitchen and my heart and taught me how to nourish my body with real food—food that's truly and naturally life sustaining and delicious.

Jewels changed the way I see a kitchen from a place to store PowerBars (my once-upon-a-time alternative to all food groups!) to a sanctuary that has become the most important room in the house, filled with sights and smells that are themselves a feast.

The beauty of spreading the secret of Jewels and Jill is it can change lives, because there's literally nothing more important to our health, happiness and success than what we put into our bodies and the energy, clarity and stamina that come as a result.

It's taken me time to learn that the key to having a great physique isn't to deprive oneself of food, but to educate oneself about the many foods our bodies crave and need as nourishment. Jewels has taught me how to take this long list of foods our bodies love and prepare them in a way that we, too, can love. B.J. (Before Jewels), I never went near a piece of fish. She was the only person who could get me to taste salmon. And now I beg her to make it and I can't eat salmon anywhere else because it never tastes like hers. She is a flavor artist with a passion for detail. And now Jewels' art form is accessible to everyone: a conscious, sensible approach to selecting and preparing guilt-free food that tastes divine!

—Jennifer Aniston

THE FAMILY CHEF

introduction

WE ARE SISTERS and we are *inseparable*. As little girls we always wanted to be together. This may have something do to with the fact that whenever we had a disagreement, our mother would send us to our room *together*—and we had to stay there until we worked it out. If we asked our mother's permission to go somewhere, she would say, "You can go if you take your sister." We shared clothes, friends and makeup. When my mom told us we were getting a little brother, we agreed to share him, too.

All these years later we are still sharing life experiences and taking each other everywhere we go.

We have been there for each other as roommates, bridesmaids and birthing coaches. Our sons (we each have one) were born six months apart. We live five minutes from each other and our husbands feel like they married two people! So when it came to choosing a profession, it made perfect sense to do something together. Since we both felt comfortable and happy cooking, we became chefs!

Why we prefer *Family Chef*

In our line of work people call themselves "personal chefs" or "private chefs," but those titles barely begin to capture all we do. We prefer Family Chef. As professional Family Chefs, we cook for our clients in their own homes and, in so doing, play an integral role in the families we serve. We are incredibly lucky to work for some of the most accomplished people in the entertainment world—powerful, strong, successful people who are defined by their positive energy, enthusiasm and achievement.

Because we cook for them in their own kitchens, just as you cook for yourself and your family at home, we see the impact that the right food, made with the right energy, can have on people and their lives. We've found that cooking is a powerful way to pass that energy from one person to another.

Which brings us to why we are writing this book. There is a secret about good cooking that we want to share with you. We put this secret into every course we make—whether we are serving a husband, next-door neighbor, studio chief, heads of state or two thousand people at the Governor's Ball at the Academy Awards: Good cooking is *not* always about being the best chef; it's about *how* you do it and the *care* you put into everything you serve. It's about bringing out the Family Chef inside of you, a chef motivated by love and passion both for food and for the people you feed.

Cooking is sexy

In our work, we see how a beautiful, fresh meal, lovingly prepared, can bring a group of family and friends together and help them enjoy one another and celebrate life. We have used food as a silent form of nurturing and comfort when words were not sufficient. We have found that the right food, carefully chosen, can tantalize and awaken dormant senses. It can drastically improve a child's behavior and give him a chance to succeed.

Prepared intentionally, food can change the course of your day—and it can change your life.

Cooking itself is sexy and smart. In the right hands, it can inspire and express as much emotion and love as music, dance or poetry. It can give you joy, hope and laughter and it can energize your soul and spirit.

In short, cooking from your heart can be one of the most loving forms of expression.

The Moroccan party

When you cook with conviction it can also save the day—or the night, as the case may be. It sure did the evening of the Moroccan party we once catered where *how* we cooked was just as important as *what* we cooked.

Now and then, our clients give the two of us as "gifts" to their friends. On this particular evening, Jewels' client had sent us over to a close friend's home to help her throw an authentic Moroccan-themed dinner for about ten people. Guests arrived at the ocean-side home on a cliff, wearing Moroccan hats, robes and heavy jewelry. They found us cooking in an open kitchen, where they could observe everything we did.

The first-course soup we served drew high praise, as did the salad. Aromatic lamb baking in individual pyramid-shaped *tagines* was just about done when we discovered that neither of us had turned on the flame under the pot of couscous.

Everybody was watching. With so many eyes on us, we couldn't show any panic. We needed to act like we *always* wait until ten minutes before the entrée is ready to start the couscous, which meant we needed another dish—immediately—to stall for time. Because the hostess had graciously cleaned out her kitchen to give us room, all we had were two blood oranges. That's it, just two pieces of fruit.

"A palate cleanser!" Jewels whispered.

"Are you crazy?" Jill said. "We can't make a palate cleanser for ten people out of *two* oranges."

The more conservative and practical-minded of us two, Jill also knows when to stifle her panic and follow Jewels' wacky lead.

Off came the orange skins. We placed two paper-thin slices on each plate in an essence of grapeseed oil with coriander and crushed mint. Black cardamom pods added a dash of contrast as a garnish.

Jill still wasn't convinced, but Jewels *believed*. "I decided, this is going to be delicious and clean and it is going to work," she remembers. She added a touch of rose water and we hoisted the plates over our heads theatrically to serve the expectant room.

The guests loved it! They were over the moon. They'd never tasted anything like it (and neither had we).

By then, the couscous was done and we were serving up the main course. It's amazing we got anything else done that evening, we were so busy congratulating each other under our breath.

At moments like those, yes, our experience comes into play. But it's the spirit with which we imbue the food we serve that wins over hearts and stomachs. We firmly believe that while you don't have to be the best chef in the room, you do have to care. The feelings of the hostess, the reputation of our client and the life of the party were at stake that night—all saved by a little passion and conviction.

Cooking by touch

It seems only natural that we grew up to feed other people for a living. It's in our blood. Our grandmother, our nana, who was raised in New Mexico, learned to cook under extraordinary circumstances. When she was just four, her mother died. The youngest of eleven, she lost four of her siblings when they were still kids, an unimaginably high toll for one family even back then. She and her siblings raised one another with the help of their father, who was blind.

In the kitchen our great-grandfather would stand at the counter and ask his children to bring him flour, salt and other ingredients. He used his sense of touch to mix them together in just the right proportions to make tortillas.

"I don't like gourmet cooking or 'this' cooking or 'that' cooking. I like good cooking."

—James Beard

Our grandmother learned to do the same, never using measuring cups or spoons. When she was teaching us how to make tortillas as kids, she would plunge her hands into the dry mixture and tell us, "It needs more baking powder." We would look at each other in amazement. Because we grew up cooking next to her, we feel—as she did—that recipes are just guides. Much of what we do today is by intuition and experimentation.

Nana was just fourteen when she moved with some of her sisters to Los Angeles and took a job as a housekeeper, nanny and cook for a Jewish family. Wonderful Molly and Simon Ruben introduced her to a new world of food. They taught her how to buy the best cuts of meat from the butcher and to make sure that butcher became a friend. They really took her in as a member of the family. We met the Rubens several times as kids; Nana stayed in touch with them until they passed away.

Between her background as a descendant of immigrants from the Mexican state of Chihuahua and her many years with the Rubens, Nana could make just about anything.

We were especially fortunate that our grandparents always lived with us. Our nana was the Queen Mother, or as we say, the Doña, of our vast, extended family. She married our grandfather, Salvador, who had eleven siblings of his own. There are so many cousins out there, we can't keep track of them all! At family reunions, it takes bleachers to hold us for the family photograph.

Our grandfather, our papa, could almost cook as well as Nana. Super-fit and super-active up until he died in his eighties, he delighted in dishes like fried frog legs, rabbit and really, really hard aged cheeses that gave off powerful aromas. He had his own specialties, like *costillitas,* little lamb riblets that he would fry up outside in a skillet on a hot plate while the women cooked indoors. As kids, we would wait in anticipation for them to be ready. They were so delicious!

Our mom, "Rocky"

Our mom, who we affectionately call "Rocky" (short for Raquel), became an amazing cook in her own right. When we entertain at any of our clients' homes, Mom usually comes and works right alongside with us. To this day, the highest praise for anything we prepare—and one that is only rarely bestowed—is a compliment from Mom.

While the two of us love to goof around in the kitchen, for Mom, cooking is serious business. When we were little, even if we were late for Jewels' music class, or if Jill had to go to the bathroom, Mom would pull the car over to the side of the road to write down every detail from a recipe on a radio cooking show. She was, and still is, a demanding perfectionist. All her cookies come out the exact same size, every time.

She has an unerring instinct, an internal alarm clock, that goes off the moment a piece of meat is done. We occasionally cut into a fillet to check its progress, but our mother never, ever would—and her dishes always come out juicy and cooked to perfection.

Although neither of us attended cooking school, we feel as though we grew up in one. We survived Rocky's kitchen, which prepared us for Wolfgang Puck's Academy Awards kitchen, our clients' Family Kitchens and many, many others.

For years, mom ran a big kitchen at our church, where we were often recruited as kitchen help. Catering was one of our first jobs and it quickly became Jewels' full-time occupation. While working for a big catering company, the Head Chef, Dave Rubel, recommended Jewels to private clients for her first jobs as a Family Chef.

One job led to another, and then another, until Jewels found herself traveling extensively with a glamorous couple, both celebrities. As the months went on they began to entertain more and more. On location in Florida, where her client was shooting a movie, Jewels was making pizza one day. In the high humidity, the rules of baking bend. As dough overflowed the pizza pans, Jewels knew she was tired, overwhelmed and terribly homesick. Very kindly, her boss asked what he could do to help make her feel better.

Jewels broke down in tears. If she could just have her sister come out to help, she told him, she could stay on location and the food would be back to snuff. He agreed.

Jill was faced with a difficult, life-changing choice. Although she was cooking part-time, flying off to Florida would probably mean quitting her stable full-time job as an administrative assistant in an office.

Jewels had a gut feeling. Once her client tasted the meals they would make *together*, they would both have a job doing what they loved. Jill arrived the next day.

We've both been cooking full-time ever since. Even when we don't work together for the same clients, we trade phone calls back and forth constantly. We're so in sync that, sometimes at the end of the day, we'll discover that we both made precisely the same dish, which neither of us had made in five years or more. Most recently it was a spicy Thai butternut squash soup with shrimp. Whenever it happens, we just shake our heads in wonder.

Nana's *capirotada*

Throughout our lives Nana did so much for all of us that, when she was ill, instinctively, our whole family and many of our cousins ground our own lives to a halt to care for her.

During those months in the hospital, day and night, she was never alone. A family member was always by her side. The two of us, our mother and our cousins decided we should be the ones to bathe her, and so we did. We massaged her legs to ease her pain and, as much as we could, cooked at home to bring her different foods to eat.

It was the least we could do. When we were kids, Nana showed us we were special by making us special dishes. When we were sick, she boiled up homemade herbal tonics. Her *capirotada*, a Mexican bread pudding, is so delicious, it could make you cry. We've never made it for our health-minded clients because it's so unbelievably rich. A syrup made of melted Mexican candy, star anise and cinnamon is poured over fried bread mixed with cheese, nuts and golden raisins and then the whole concoction bakes until it fills the home with its sweet aroma.

Our grandmother used to make *capirotada* every year for Easter and it was one of the best things about the holiday.

After she died, the loss was so tremendous for our family no one knew what to say or do. We came home from the hospital, devastated, and slowly followed Mom's lead into the kitchen. The kitchen drawer where Mom keeps aprons seemed to produce an endless supply. Cousin after cousin joined us, strapping yet another apron around their waists. Mom started with a big pot of beans on the stove top. Jill started warming tamales. Flour tortillas spread out on the counter. Dish after dish, we cooked slowly, not talking much, not even knowing exactly what we were making. We knew that, if she could, Nana would have done just this to comfort us.

After a while we started telling stories and laughing as more and more people came to the house. Cooking together we found a way to start healing ourselves.

A few months later, our mother made the first *capirotada* since Nana died. The warm, sweet flavors made us feel that she was still with us.

A kitchen filled with family

Our experience of family has been such an intensely rewarding one that we can't help but want to perpetuate it and share it with others. This is why we prefer to work in Family Kitchens as Family Chefs. For us, the most satisfying and delicious cooking happens in a home filled with a family.

Although we grew up in a very traditional family structure, we have encountered many very loving families out there that don't look a thing like ours. We've come to believe that families need not conform to any traditional model. The best families, of all configurations, are composed of people who spend their lives together and devote themselves to one another's growth and happiness.

Breaking molds suits us because we like breaking rules. Most days we don't wear chef whites when we cook. We don't mind having the dogs and the kids underfoot—even when we entertain (seriously; you'll soon learn why!). And we don't even like the word "recipe." Really, we think recipes shouldn't be taken as gospel but thought of as good ideas that worked for someone else and may or may not work for you. In other words, in life, as in cooking, feel free to improvise!

That means Family Chefs may cook for one spouse and no children, or for a group of close friends, or for a same-sex partner. And they may even cook just for themselves.

We believe healthy families begin with strong and healthy individuals like these. The best Family Chefs (and this doesn't always describe us when we are busy, busy, busy) remember to care for themselves first. They remember that nurturing their bodies with good food is the exact opposite of selfish. Family Chefs often start a meal by preparing something they want that is delicious and healthy and sharing it with the people they love.

Variety!

When people ask us, "What is your style or specialty?" we say, "Variety!" We believe in experimentation and trying new things. We have to! We've learned how essential this is through cooking for our clients at home—you don't want them to feel like they are eating in the same restaurant every night! Like you, our challenge is to satisfy the same eaters day after day. Our clients have traveled the globe and savored the most exceptional delicacies. They often ask us to re-create a dish they discovered on a trip. You can expose your family (and yourself) to other countries and cultures in a small way just by preparing and serving some of the simple recipes in this book and you will keep them excited about what's put in front of them.

People also ask us, "What do you cook for your boss?" Our answer: We cook the way we cook for our own families by using fresh, unprocessed food with a diversity of flavors and textures that keep their attention.

Once you learn what to buy and how to combine those ingredients, your confidence will grow. You may find yourself riffing off recipes with culinary instincts you didn't even know you had! Our goal is to give you a foundation of diverse recipes. Once you learn them, you can then *make them your own.*

While we agree on the importance of cooking with intention, we each bring a different style to *how* we go about it, in the same way every Family Chef has a unique style.

Jill is the practical and straightforward one. She makes no fuss while effortlessly creating a beautiful plate that is both simple and delicious. Jewels, on the other hand, tends to make things a bit more complex with a few extra steps and special ingredients. She loves layering flavors and textures and believes it's all about the details.

For some of our recipes we have included two versions—one from Jewels and one from Jill—to give you more than one option and to inspire you to make your own alterations.

Cooking with intention

Whichever kind of Family Chef you may be, we hope to inspire you to bring a new sense of discovery, play and fun to the meals you make for yourself and the people you love. At a time when many families struggle to find time and activities to share, cooking is the most natural place to start. Eating is a necessity, but it shouldn't be drudgery. Approaching each meal as a Family Chef can turn eating together daily into play and celebrations while creating meaningful bonds.

We've designed this book to help you bring *intention* to your cooking, to bring your awareness to the environment in which you cook and to make you more conscious of your state of mind when you are creating in the kitchen—all of which we believe has a tangible effect on what ends up on the plate.

Your power as a Family Chef

Perhaps our greatest hope is to awaken people to the power that the passionate Family Chef wields. Cooking delicious food together can unite families like nothing else. We don't think it's a stretch to say that, at times, great Family Chefs can even save their families. Cooking together can be a healthy and fun way to create and sustain those "ties that bind," as the expression goes. That's what we've found. We're so fortunate to have such strong family bonds and cooking together is a big part of why we do. Even though we kids are now adults, on any given day, we might be back in Rocky's kitchen—or she and the rest of our family might be in one of ours.

Staying conscious of the gift

There are so many talented chefs out there. We believe our fruitful careers blossomed out of our passion, enjoyment and gratitude for what we do—a passion we believe we can pass on to anyone willing to bring a little love to their cooking. We've discovered that the "secret" to good food is to stay conscious of the gift you are giving—and receiving—with every minute of effort.

As you see the fulfillment in the eyes of your own family members, you will realize that you have not only nourished their bodies and minds, but you have fed their souls.

inspiration

So, **HOW DOES** a Family Chef stay inspired?

No one knows the challenge of having to be creative, day after day, as well as the Family Chef. With the same people sitting at our tables for every meal every day, year after year, we need constant sources of new inspiration.

What works for us is to stay open to new ideas—from just about any source. Ask your fishmonger or butcher how he would prepare the best fish or meat of the day. Visit a specialty market or an ethnic store that carries ingredients you have never used; we have spent hours in these spots just exploring and asking questions. Read through cookbooks; we have a huge and ever-expanding collection of books we page through every day.

Why we love Jamie

One chef and cookbook author who especially inspires us—and who we aspire to emulate—is none other than Jamie Oliver. We are so blessed to know Jamie. He is such a generous guy and we've learned so much just by watching and listening to him.

Jamie is a model for us because he's one chef who, we believe, understands the power he wields with food—and uses that power for good! He really knows the impact that good food can have on every individual. He works so hard to share this knowledge. Through his cookbooks and shows, he is succeeding at changing the way people eat today. He's raised the level of consciousness about the importance of healthy food in the U.K., where he lives and works. He's on a mission to get junk out of school meals and to teach kids all he knows about great food and healthy, delicious cooking.

He's a chef who cooks with his heart and soul, and for that reason, he's a hero to us. He inspires us to go out and share the good news.

Inspiration is everywhere

Inspiration is everywhere. Every friend or stranger we meet might give us a new idea about preparing a dish in a new way. Hearing someone speak another language has prompted us to make food from a different country. Eating out inspires us to try to re-create our exciting new discoveries.

Simply changing the scenery can help. Eat outside or in the park, something our huge family loves to do; we fit better outside than in restaurants! Don't be afraid to move things around and use your coffee table to serve an Indian or Japanese meal. Visit a cooking store and ask yourself what you could make to fill that unique plate or bowl. Watch a cooking show or movies about cooking while you prepare meals.

Above all, don't forget to cook with your heart and soul, which will bring every meal to life. Bring eyes of gratitude to the kitchen as you strap on your apron. Remember how fortunate we all are just to be asking the simple question: "What will we have for dinner tonight?"

the family kitchen

NOW AND THEN somebody says to us, "You girls should open a restaurant!" Occasionally they offer to invest money and back us. Before anyone gets carried away, we say, "Thanks, but no, thanks." For most top chefs, opening a restaurant is the ultimate dream. But it's not ours. In our view, nothing compares to the Family Kitchen.

The reasons are simple. We want to cook in a place that feels like home. We feel happiest when surrounded by family. And we both feel we *need* to know the people we are cooking for.

When we were growing up, our Family Kitchen was the place that held us all together. Everything happened there. Along with cooking and eating, there were lectures, debates, celebrations, lots of laughs and sometimes tears. In our family home, everyone gravitated to our kitchen.

The feeling of comfort and consistency in our Family Kitchen kept bringing us all together. By showing you how to create meals like a Family Chef, this is what we want to help you create in your home.

The Academy Awards Governor's Ball

Although we are, first and foremost, Family Chefs, it's not that we haven't cooked for strangers in high-pressure, high-visibility settings. Given the people we work for, and their love of entertaining, we cater events all the time—in homes and in unique venues—that demand cuisine of equal or superior quality to that of the best five-star restaurants.

Back before Wolfgang Puck had started his own catering company, in the early nineties, we got drafted into helping him serve more than two thousand people who attended the Academy Awards Governor's Ball at the Shrine Auditorium in downtown Los Angeles. Jewels, who was only twenty-five at the time, oversaw the entrée kitchen and Jill, just twenty-two, ran the appetizer kitchen. We wore headsets to stay in constant communication with each other throughout the night and keep up a smooth flow of dishes streaming out the kitchen door. We swear it felt like five hundred people were working in that kitchen!

Lucky for us, when you grow up in a large family, you learn how to deal with crowds. In Mom's kitchen at home, it seems like she was always cooking up a feast for twenty people and ordering everyone about in the process. We've each cultivated our own styles of motivating large groups of people to cook as one. Jill inspires confidence and respect with her own brand of quiet authority. Jewels, on the other hand, is the outright bossy one. At the Governor's Ball, Jewels climbed up onto overturned milk crates to bark orders through a bullhorn.

As she worked that night, Jill couldn't help feeling she was in over her head. "I was thinking, once again Jewels has gone and told someone I could do something—*that I've never done before!*"

But the evening came out beautifully (and we came back to do it again in following years).

Later that night, driving home, we could not believe how many people we had served! It was the first of many truly humongous kitchens we have worked and learned in.

The mystery chef from Woodside

We've found we can learn so much just by watching other people cook. Catering major events gave us the chance to observe some of the world's other top chefs at work. It was so inspiring!

Especially at the start of our careers. In our early twenties, when we were just starting out, we were particularly affected by watching a young woman whose name we didn't even know. Together the two of us had moved from the suburbs where we'd grown up to the Westside of Los Angeles. We rented an apartment together, catered part-time and walked every morning together to strategize about our futures. "We've gotta get out more!" we'd tell each other. We'd save up our money all week, put on cute outfits and go out for a nice meal on the weekends. Often, we'd end up at a wonderful restaurant that (sadly) doesn't exist anymore called Woodside in Brentwood.

Woodside had an open kitchen and a very cute blond woman who seemed to be running the show. We guessed she was about the same age as we were. Especially when we were feeling low, we loved watching her as she swirled sauces and shucked oysters. "Look at her," we'd say, deeply impressed. "*We* could do that." We would go home reinvigorated.

Fast-forward several years and we became friends with Kevin, who ran the floor (the dining room) at the Governor's Ball. One day he introduced us to his fiancée,

Louise, who was also a chef. Louise quickly became a good friend to both of us. We hung out all the time; Jewels was even in the room when her first baby was born. After Louise became a mom, Kevin wanted to help her leave the bustle of restaurant work to become a private chef. He asked if we could help. As we were looking over her résumé, we saw she'd been the executive chef at Woodside. No wonder it felt as though we'd always known her!

Jewels called Louise on the phone. She cried as she told Louise how much she had inspired us when we were younger. It was wonderful getting the chance to return the favor and help her make the transition to becoming a Family Chef, doing what we love best.

"You got me"

If we had to sum up our purpose in life, we'd say it's *to make people happy with food*. The ideal place to ensure we do so is the Family Kitchen. But, wherever you cook, keeping people well nourished and healthy isn't the easiest undertaking when you cook for people who are busy all the time. If you're like most people today, you know what we're talking about!

A big part of being a successful Family Chef is learning to read the moods and anticipate the needs of your family members. One of Jewels' former longtime clients is so busy that, although he loves to eat, he didn't make time to do it! Enticing him to the table took real creativity. On particularly hectic days, Jewels would hear him dashing about upstairs and know he was probably running a little behind. Working stealthily downstairs, she would fill the house with tantalizing smells of delicious foods, hoping he would catch his first whiff before he descended.

As he dashed past the kitchen saying, "I'm sorry, Jewels. That smells great, but I just don't have time to eat," she would nonchalantly set a hot plate of food on the counter right under his nose.

"Oh, man," he'd say, stopping in his tracks for a closer look. "You got me."

Unable to resist, he'd take just enough time to polish off a quick meal.

When he thanked her, she told him something we really believe is true: "If we make sure you are nourished, it only makes our lives better." When you think of it, the same is true in every family home.

Sure he was five minutes late. But he'd leave so much happier and in such a better place. "On days like that, I really feel I've done my job," Jewels says.

Reading plates

One of the things we both love to do with our work families—and our own families—is *stretch* them beyond their comfort zones. We've been called "plate readers" because we pay attention to what our family members *actually* eat, as opposed to what they *say* they eat.

Jill's husband, Simon, used to tell her he didn't like cilantro, but she noticed he ate all the fresh salsa she made even though it was filled with it. She realized the secret was that, if she chopped up the cilantro, it was OK. Simple solution. Now it seems like she puts cilantro in everything and he loves it. Jewels was once cooking for a studio head who told her he didn't like Mexican food. That pushed a button! One night, she couldn't resist preparing that most Mexican of Mexican dishes, chiles rellenos. Walking into the dining room, she told him, "I know you don't like Mexican food, so I've got a backup dinner in the kitchen, but do me a favor and please try this." Placing it before him she went back to the kitchen only to have him summon her back in a few minutes later. "I don't know if I'm more mad because you made Mexican food," he said, "or because I really love this."

The kids in Jill's clients' home used to say over and over again that they didn't like fish. Jill understood. When she first started working as a private chef, she recoiled at the thought of preparing fish because it was never her favorite food—that is, until Jewels made the most delicious fresh fish and changed Jill's mind forever.

Just as she'd been won over, Jill resolved to turn her clients into fish lovers, too, especially because she now believes that the omega oils in fish should be a part of everyone's diet. For one of her clients' sons, Jill started stuffing the California rolls that he loves full of baked salmon instead of crab and put them in his lunch box. Now—surprise!—he loves fish as much as she does.

So, what do you *really* think?

As a Family Chef, you've got to be strong. If you cook at a restaurant and the guests don't like the food, they might never come back again and you might never hear why. When *our* audience doesn't like the food we make, the feedback is immediate. The best Family Chefs learn to take criticism happily. It's not pleasant, but it's necessary. In fact, rather than shying away from criticism, we ask for it. We don't want our family members to hide their true opinions. To know their palates well, we need to know what they think about everything they eat.

The better we know someone's unique taste in food, the better we can serve them. One of Jewels' clients used to tell her she didn't like Indian food because she didn't like the way it smells. Jewels thought that one over a bit. She knew her client well enough to guess just which spices, to her, probably produced that unsavory aroma. Without making a fuss, Jewels began to prepare Indian dishes, but omitting a couple of seasonings. A few months later, she overheard her client telling a friend how much she liked Indian food.

Mission accomplished.

"I better get rid of my 'stuff'"

Family Chefs must be strong in another way, too. We take cooking with love seriously, which means we take responsibility for the state of mind we bring into the kitchen, no matter what is happening around us. Sometimes cooking can pull us out of a funk, but some funks are worse than others. Many years ago, Jewels was going through a challenging period in her personal life and going to work every day was difficult.

"Finally I started thinking, wow, I better get rid of my 'stuff,'" Jewels remembers.

She began to focus even more closely on doing her job as a Family Chef well, and it ended up helping her, too.

"It allowed me to really, really let go of what I was experiencing," she remembers. "I discovered that, when I came back to myself, I felt so much better because I had been in service to someone else. Because you are nourishing and giving, it gives you a lot of power and can make you stronger. I would see how I had cared for others and I would realize I needed to do that for myself."

Over time, Jewels' clients quietly returned the favor. In their own ways, they cared for her, too, helping her to recapture her spark. We've found that when we care for others, they can't help but do the same.

Doing time

In our opinion, one quality true of every Family Kitchen is a sense of community. In our family home, that meant that everybody—and we mean everybody—pitched in. If you happened to walk through on your way to the bathroom, Nana would give you a job. If you wanted to eat, you had to put in your time.

As little kids, we shucked corn or pulled the tops off of strawberries. Often the men stoked the barbecues or did the washing and carrying. They also competed to see who could stir the *massa* (cornmeal dough) long and hard enough until it floated in water, which signaled it was, finally, ready to be wrapped in corn husks to make tamales. Our father doesn't cook. But that doesn't mean he doesn't pitch in. The son of hardy Midwestern folks from Indiana, he grew up on a ranch with horses in the California town of Arcadia, where everyone did chores. When he married into Mom's sprawling Mexican-American clan, our very-gringo dad found his own way to keep the Family Kitchen humming. It seems as though he is always heading off to the store to get another forgotten ingredient, washing dishes or hauling a sack of chilis in the back door. Believe us, the man knows what he's doing; he eats exceptionally well.

When a kid saved the day

Having everyone pitch in is our philosophy in our clients' homes, too. That is, to different degrees. You'll never catch Jill handing a task off to the man of the house in her clients' homes, but Jewels, on the other hand, is fearless.

"I am always amazed what Jewels gets away with," Jill said, remembering the time when Jewels got a studio head to *happily* make her a drink. With Jewels' infectious enthusiasm, working in the kitchen feels like joining a party.

We like getting everyone involved while gabbing and goofing around in front of the stove. You know how, at parties, everyone seems to end up in the kitchen? It's no different in our clients' homes. The pull of the Family Kitchen is too irresistible and we like to make it the most engaging place for people to gather.

"Everything you see
I owe to spaghetti."

—Sophia Loren

We know otherwise friendly chefs who are so serious about their cooking that their personalities turn almost militaristic as they work. No matter the venue, they're always wearing their snappy chef whites. And God forgive any child who wanders into the kitchen and sticks a finger into the soup.

We couldn't be more different. We like people to sample food while it's cooking or being whipped together. When a bored child leans against the fridge, we give him food to prep and set him up with his own workstation. This isn't charity. After a little training, kids become good little sous-chefs and make our jobs both easier and fun!

In her quiet, efficient way, Jill used to think she could save time by preparing every meal herself. She knew exactly what she was doing, she figured, and could do it faster than anyone else anyway. But, after working alongside Jewels preparing countless dinners and parties in clients' homes, she realized that, even if a little teaching is involved, it's always faster in the end—and so much more fun—when lots of people pitch in.

Rather than hinder our progress, sometimes our clients' kids become indispensable. Like the time Jill was preparing an elegant meal for her client, who was hosting a table full of famous actors, producers and directors. As the evening rolled along, her client's nine-year-old son—bored by all the grown-up talk—came into the kitchen to hang out with Jill. She was prepping a mouthwatering chocolate soufflé for dessert when the power suddenly flickered out. Festive candles restored light to the dining room table but, with an electric oven, Jill's plans for the meal's finale were cooked. "Oh my gosh!" Jill recalled thinking. "*What* am I going to do for dessert?"

"I know!" her client's son said, shining a flashlight in her face. "We can make root beer floats!"

Jill mulled it over for a half second. "Actually," she told him, "that's a great idea!"

The guests slurped them up and pronounced the idea genius. The real genius, in our opinion, is keeping the family in the kitchen.

Screwups

This brings us to a subject near and dear to the heart of every person who cooks: screwups. When you cook, they're gonna happen. The best Family Chefs know screwups are part of the equation. They learn to laugh them off and move on.

Seriously, what's the other option?

So many chefs are as famous for their tantrums as they are for their cuisine. Sure, we get upset from time to time, but it doesn't help matters when we do. You may think a particular screwup is a disaster but, really, it's not.

Take the time Jill was helping Jewels prep for a baby shower Jewels' client was throwing for forty guests. The night before, Jill had baked four dozen tiny vanilla cupcakes. After she'd gone to bed, her husband, Simon, came home, starved as usual. In addition to working hard every day, Simon is a surfer and capable of scarfing down an ungodly amount of food all at once. The little cupcakes reminded him of a dessert his grandmother used to make and he happily devoured more than half of them before turning in.

When Jill woke up the next day, Simon said, "I ate your cakes. They were beautiful!" She looked at him, stunned.

"What?" he said, catching her meaning. "I didn't see a note saying I couldn't."

Sure, Jill could have thrown a fit, but how would that have helped? Instead she worked at double speed the next morning to bake several new batches. (And now she puts notes on everything she doesn't want Simon to eat.)

Another time, Jewels spent *two days* working on a beautiful veal stock, simmering and checking it—did we mention it was for *two days*—in preparation for a very important dinner. A new kitchen assistant was helping out that day. Jewels asked her to carefully pour the stock through cheesecloth and a strainer and return it to her so it could be finished. Off went the assistant. She returned to present Jewels with a bowl of bones and soggy, overcooked vegetables. The meticulously prepared stock had been strained, all right, straight down the kitchen sink!

It is during times like these when we all have a choice. We can yell, scream and order everyone out of the kitchen. Or we can dig deep and find a solution . . . and a sense of humor. Often, at these "worst" moments, we look at each other and just crack up—because we can!

When you are the Family Chef you need to remember why you are there—to feed, nurture and show your love. So, if you find your assistant (or child) has innocently used sugar instead of salt, smile and keep some perspective, remember how lucky you are to have fresh food to cook with, assistants (or relatives) to help and the chance to prepare and enjoy delicious meals with the people you love.

To be honest, Rocky often comes to our rescue when things go awry. Each of the Family Kitchens we cook in is immensely enriched by the fact that our mother still cooks daily back in the home where we grew up.

You can guess what Jewels did after she realized that veal stock had vanished down the drain. She called Mom to see if she happened to have any homemade stock in the freezer. Lucky for Jewels (and her clients), Rocky and the original Family Kitchen came through again.

Here are some basics to help you create a Family Kitchen of your own.

The equipment

There's no mystery here: Use what you have. You probably already own the very few basic items we believe the best home cooking requires. We strongly suggest at least one essential: a very sharp six- to eight-inch knife. When you cut with a really great knife, you'll be surprised at how much easier it is to cook! Other than your time, it will be the best investment you make in your kitchen.

Jill's kitchen basics

- At least one really sharp chopping knife
- Cutting board (she is partial to a good old wood cutting board)
- Heavy-bottom skillet
- Large stockpot
- Metal spatula
- Metal tongs
- Wooden spoon
- Large mixing bowls
- Good blender or hand blender
- Salad spinner

"Pull up a chair. Take a taste. Come join us. Life is so endlessly delicious."

—Ruth Reichl

Jewels' kitchen extras

- Clear plastic jars to store lentils, rice, beans. If you can see all your ingredients, they will inspire you to use them.
- Metallic spice containers with glass lids and magnetic bottoms enable you to keep spices readily available and beautifully displayed on the side of your refrigerator.
- Asian mandolin for the thinnest slicing (use with caution)
- Fine strainer for soups and to drain very small grains

Dry-good staples

Keep your pantry stocked with the following:

- *Organic chicken stock*
  If you don't have any, you can always swap in vegetable stock or even plain water.

- *Extra-virgin olive oil*
  They all taste different, so sample different makers to find your favorites.

- *Canned tomatoes*

  We prefer San Marzano because they tend to be the most ripe at the time of canning.

- *Dried lentils*

  It's amazing how many delicious dishes include lentils. They keep for a long time and take just minutes to prepare. They can accompany or star in almost any dish and are so good for you, too.

- *Dried and/or canned beans*

- *Rice*

- *Onions (if you are Jill) or shallots (if you are Jewels)*

- *Sea salt or kosher salt*

- *A pepper mill*

JEWELS' SMART IDEA

I love different kinds of salts and peppers. I keep lots of little bowls of beautiful salts around: red salts, chunky grey salts and jet-black "lava salt," which is salt combined with purified volcanic charcoal, a natural detoxifier. I pour different peppercorn varieties into different clear pepper mills so I can easily spot the ones I want to use. I love labeling everything in my kitchen with an understated label maker I picked up at an office-supply store. The joy of being organized!

JILL'S SMART IDEA

Take all the caps off your different oils and vinegars. Replace them with liquor-pouring spouts. Doing so will really save time while you cook, allowing you to add these ingredients with just one hand while you stir a pot or sauté vegetables. Also, keep the oils and vinegars away from the heat. They'll stay fresh longer if they are cool.

Fresh basics

We love food that tastes fresh, light and alive. Using fresh herbs and lemons or limes is a simple way to brighten a dish and make flavors pop. If possible, keep the following on hand:

- Parsley
- Mint
- Basil
- Cilantro
- Rosemary
- Thyme
- Lemons and limes

Grow small herb pots in your kitchen. Not only will you keep the freshest herbs handy; they make your kitchen look—and smell—beautiful and inviting.

The workspace

Clear counters will clear your mind. If you keep the kitchen counters as clutter-free as possible, the extra room will translate into a user-friendly, enjoyable environment to get some creative cooking done. If your family uses the kitchen counters as a dumping zone for papers and keys, find another repository for these items. It may take a little while to retrain everyone in the family to unload their junk elsewhere, but be persistent. Eventually they will get the idea. You're creating sacred space for family meals. And you may even have room for more people to help out!

Every day you cook you will begin to establish a routine that can be a great source of comfort. We begin preparing each meal the same way by employing a little restaurant trick: We put on an apron and tie the strings so that two kitchen towels hang on each side of our bodies. Those towels come in handy when picking up hot pans, wiping our hands and brushing crumbs off the cutting board. The next step in our routine is pulling out the cutting board and knife and then laying the rest of our favorite cooking implements nearby.

Jewels assembles all the meal's ingredients by displaying them in a favorite basket or bowl before she begins. Surrounding herself with the sights and smells that make her happy motivates and inspires her. When she first started her current job, her new client watched Jewels with bemusement, assuming she was putting on a bit of a show. Over time, as she got to know Jewels, she realized that Jewels was indeed putting on a show—just for herself, for her own pleasure and to accentuate the sensual pleasure of making the day's meals.

In her efficient way, Jill pulls out only those ingredients she is using at the moment because it makes her happier to spend less time fussing and more time cooking.

Basic guidelines

- **Keep your work space clean**

    Place your garbage can under or next to the counter where you've set up your cutting board so you can easily sweep carrot tops and crumbs into the trash and keep them off the floor. Your cleanup will be faster.

- **Set up workstations for your helpers**

    Give each family member, no matter how old, an area of his or her own to work on assigned projects. They will also be responsible for cleaning up their areas after they complete each task. By assigning spaces, the busiest restaurants keep large numbers of people working in an orderly fashion in the same kitchen at the same time. Kids will appreciate the responsibility and feel proud to have a place and a role of their own.

- **Cook outside**

    Few families think to cook outside regularly, but we love to cook outside! When a large group of people cooks together, adding the outdoors gives us much more room. Outside is a great "station" for kids, especially for messy jobs. You can't beat the feeling of working on a cutting board in the fresh air.

- **Safety rule**

    We have a traffic rule in the kitchen: Call it out! When you pass behind someone else in a busy kitchen—with or without food in your hands—let them know you are there by announcing "Behind you" or "Behind you with a hot pan" or "Behind you with a full tray." By observing these traffic rules, we avoid an untold number of collisions and spills. Calling it out ensures a safe cooking environment for everybody.

- **Everybody cleans up!**

    We really believe in this! If everyone pitches in, the work goes faster and the fun of shared activity continues. Cleaning up is as much a part of cooking as chopping or sautéing—and it can be just as much fun! Play music, sing, talk about your day and continue to enjoy one another's company.

> **About the ingredients.** We want you to be excited to use exotic spices and ingredients—not intimidated! So, if you see something in our recipes you don't recognize, just go to our *Resource* section on pages 299–310. We've listed online stores where you can buy just about everything you need to make the recipes in this book quickly and, in many cases, cheaply!

THE FAMILY KITCHEN

smart shopping

THE FOLLOWING IS one of the simplest and most important pieces of practical advice we have for you in this entire book: If you do your shopping well, your work as a Family Chef is more than halfway done.

Did you get that? If not, stop and reread the previous paragraph because it couldn't be more important.

In fact, it's so important that if you can grasp it, you will transform every meal you make for everyone you cook for, for the rest of your life!

Because this is such a simple principle, it's amazing to us how few people understand or have even heard of it. But, to tell the truth, it took us a lot of trial and error to really put it into practice ourselves.

Here's how most people who cook ignore this important rule daily (as we used to): They get an idea about what they want to make for dinner, head out to the market, buy ingredients listed in a recipe and then come home to fix the meal.

Sound familiar? Contrary to popular belief, if you cook this way, you will never make exceptional meals on a regular basis.

Instead, you've got to reverse the formula so that the creative process really begins not while reading a recipe, but when you step into the market. Every day we head out to our favorite spots on a hunt for only those meats, fish, vegetables and fruits that are in season and the most fresh and delicious on that day.

No matter what recipe ideas we start out with, we make dishes that can be prepared with the freshest, seasonal ingredients available right then. This means we've got to be flexible. And it means our clients—and our families—have learned to be flexible, too.

Bite before you buy

Jill is a big fan of summer corn on the cob and loves to make it for large gatherings. When in season, super-fresh corn bursts with such sweetness that it doesn't need butter, salt or pepper. But starchy corn that tastes like cardboard is such a disappointment. Rather than take a chance by buying a dozen ears of corn that look good—but may not be—Jill invests in buying a single ear. She'll take a few bites in the market before deciding whether to toss more in the basket.

Or say our client has requested rack of lamb one evening. At the butcher's, we'll only buy some if it looks amazing and if the butcher confirms for us that it is. If it isn't, then we search for something better. "What's the best thing you've got for us today?" we ask, or "What are you making tonight?"

Often, and especially because we are friends with our butchers, they tell us about something that just came in. It might be filet mignon or a leg of lamb that's still out back.

We ask them to bring it in and take a look.

Often, on the way home, we call our clients to let them know the menu for the evening meal has changed. They've come to trust us when we do.

Leave it to Mother Nature

People think we're being modest when we confess that, sometimes, we don't feel we should take credit for a great meal. But we mean it. Do your shopping well and Mother Nature does the hard work.

We like fancy, complex dishes as well as the next person, but sometimes simple is best. Slice up a just-picked homegrown heirloom tomato along with a beautiful ripe avocado and some fresh parsley. Drizzle with olive oil and add leaves of basil off the potted herb plant over your sink—and you're done!

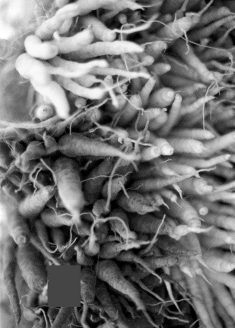

Often, we use just a dab of olive oil, salt and pepper on the freshest possible fillet of fish and grill it lightly. For a side dish, we might use Tuscan kale, also called *cavalo nero* or black kale, which is so good for you and just delicious when super-fresh. At the first bite, our clients give us all the credit.

Why bother correcting them?

Paying attention

Through trial and error, we've learned not to buy anything we feel a little funny about. It wasn't always this way. Jill remembers being so bent on making a certain dish or using a particular ingredient that she bought something without ensuring it met the highest standards. As she rolled her cart toward the checkout stand, she'd find herself feeling a bit uncomfortable. If she did take that ingredient home, often she'd be back to replace it a few hours later.

Today, if the fishmonger has wrapped up a piece of fish that Jill feels a bit doubtful about, she will unwrap it and smell it before she puts it in her cart. Fish should never smell fishy or funny in any way. It should smell clean like the ocean. If it doesn't, back it goes.

Social shopping

Shopping with Jewels used to drive Jill crazy. It seemed as though Jewels would stop and talk with every single person who worked in the store. She'd flirt and tell jokes and they'd do the same. Trying not to roll her eyes, Jill would be thinking, "Can we just *finish* shopping already so we can get home and cook?" It seemed like such a giant waste of time.

Then one day, we went together to Santa Monica Seafood, the most popular spot for fresh fish on the Westside of Los Angeles. It was packed with a half-hour-long line. After we took our number, one of the salesmen recognized Jewels and motioned her over. "What do you need?" he asked in a low voice. "I'll help you out."

Jill figured out then that Jewels' social shopping saves time in the long run. It produces the best deals from salespeople who have become friends and are eager to please. And it's so much more fun.

"Now," Jill says, "I talk to everybody when I shop."

Often we start our mornings shopping together, juggling babies and exclaiming over herbs at the farmers' market in Santa Monica. We fill our rolling carts and hand bags to overflowing with purslane, Japanese shiso, maitake mushrooms, yellow and orange

raspberries, orangequats and onion sprouts with their decorative black seeds. Jewels, who is crazy about tomatoes, particularly loves the pinkish Japanese tomatoes, especially for smoking or grilling. They're ridiculously juicy and the skin is so soft that the flavors seep right through. Jill, for her part, is a big fan of pineapple heirloom tomatoes and fanciful zebra tomatoes, with their bright green and yellow stripes.

The farmers' market is truly a feast for the eyes. By evening, most chefs are off in their separate worlds making dinner. But, at the farmers' market, everyone gets a chance to say hello in a gorgeous, laid-back setting. We love running into other cooks and great local chefs we admire, a couple of whom we count as friends, like Sherry Yard, one of the most amazing pastry chefs we know. It's fun to kibbitz with Dave and Karl, the mushroom guys, and our friend Romeo, whose entire family works at our favorite produce stand. Even more fun is the crowd itself: elderly people carrying home precious ingredients for their evening dinner, lots of people in their workout clothes, clusters of culinary students in their conspicuous chef whites and tons of moms with their babies. Recently, we saw a tiny kid sharing his stroller with bags and bags of fresh produce. Red leafy lettuce poked out right in front of him as he grabbed off clumps to eat, covering his face and hands with messy bits and pieces. You gotta love the sight of kids gorging on greens.

Striking gold

Wherever you shop, you have the power to see shopping as a chore or as a fun outing. It is completely up to you.

Our mom had an incredible knack for making grocery shopping seem like a trip to Disneyland. When we were kids she would sometimes drive us hours to visit a special market. Her excitement upon finding a unique ingredient, a great cut of meat or beautiful produce was contagious. We all felt we'd struck gold. Today, we shop with the same sense of excitement and anticipation.

If you are lucky enough to have a farmers' market near you, take your kids shopping. They will love being outside with you, exploring. The unique offerings there will help open your mind and put the freshest food on your table.

Why you *want* to shop with your kids

Whichever market you visit, give each member of your family a specific job. Kids can take the responsibility for picking out the best apples or the freshest head of lettuce.

Create a reliable routine by letting them do their job every time they shop with you. If you do this with older kids or your partner, you can cut your shopping time in half!

It does take more time to shop with little ones, but if you talk to your kids about different foods while you shop and let them experience the scents, colors and textures for themselves, you will spend less time trying to convince them to eat meals prepared with those ingredients later.

Another advantage to delegating shopping: If you send others out to help with the shopping, they sometimes come back with something you didn't even know they liked!

Here are some specific shopping guidelines:

Choosing produce

When you pick out fresh produce, always look for fruits and vegetables that are in season. And don't forget to smell!

If a peach doesn't smell like a peach, then it probably doesn't taste that great, either, so try something else instead. It's that simple. One ripe Japanese or heirloom tomato is worth an entire bag of cheap hard tomatoes that are white on the inside and tasteless.

It is surprising how drastically someone's preferences can change when they start eating quality food. Our clients sometimes say things like, "I don't usually like spinach but this is delicious." Little do they know that we didn't do anything more than buy a really, really fresh bunch.

Many people think they don't like green veggies because they have only tasted them from a can. This holds especially true for kids. We know it is not always possible to find the fresh produce you have in mind to use, but once you master a few simple recipes, it will become easier to get creative with fresher items.

Tips for buying produce
- If possible, shop at a farmers' market.
- Buy in season.
- Buy organic.
- Buy local.
- Smell and touch before you buy.
- If it doesn't look good, ask your grocer what has just come in.
- Ask your grocer for a taste. He or she will cut open a sample for you to try.
- If you don't see what you want, ask your grocer to order it. Jill does this often—especially when she cannot find *cavalo nero*!

Meats and poultry

When it comes to meat, your best bet is to try different cuts of meat from different butchers. If you don't want to break the bank, try a less expensive cut of meat, but always make sure it's fresh, fresh, fresh.

Chicken is such a widely used meat that we are surprised when people don't take the time to buy the best quality. Because our jobs sometimes involve travel and take us to other countries, we've learned some important things about poultry. In Paris and London, we were amazed to discover how much more free-range and organic chicken is available. Europeans are much farther ahead of us Americans in this department.

Air-chilling poultry is now de rigueur in most of Europe. You can find air-chilled poultry in the United States, too, if you look for it at specialty stores—and we recommend you do. While most processors slaughter their poultry and then dunk them in chlorinated water, "air-chilled" birds are eviscerated and then chilled in cold rooms to keep bacteria at a minimum. Chicken that is air-chilled is so much more flavorful, neither slimy nor watery. The color of the meat is better and the skin is crisper after roasting.

However, just because poultry is labeled "free-range," "organic" or even "air-chilled" doesn't guarantee you will like it. Some brands are just tastier than others. We encourage you to try different ones and choose your favorites, as we do.

Tips for buying meat and poultry

- If you can, shop at a local independent butcher or specialty market.
- Try different markets. Not all brands are the same, so compare.
- Buy organic.
- Get to know your butcher.
- Ask him or her how to prepare different cuts.
- Remember that if it looks old, it probably is.
- Try to buy air-chilled poultry.
- Look for meat that is moist and red, which indicates it has been freshly cut. Drier cuts are not fresh (aged meats are the exception to this rule).
- Remember you don't have to buy prepackaged meats, which are cut to minimize cost to the eye of the shopper. If you want a thicker cut, ask your butcher to custom cut you a piece. Few shoppers take advantage of this option.
- If possible, smell before you purchase.
- Even if you prefer to eat skinless poultry, buy it with the skin on. Cooking with the skin on retains moisture and flavor; the skin protects the flesh during cooking.

Fish

As you've probably figured out from the way Jill shops, the most basic rule about buying fish is that, if it smells bad, it is bad. Fish should smell neither fishy nor like ammonia. Because we never compromise on the quality of the fish, our clients want to eat it often. Quality translates to freshness, though not necessarily to cost; sometimes a fish priced at twenty dollars a pound isn't as fresh as another at seven ninety-nine a pound. The fresher option is *always* better. If you must use canned or frozen fish (emphasis on *if you must*), then make sure it was fresh before it was canned or frozen. You can smell and taste the difference! We also strongly believe in buying fish that is *wild*, as opposed to farm-raised, whenever possible.

If you take time to seek out a great local fishmonger, you'll be more inspired than ever to regularly incorporate this "must-eat" food into your family menus.

Here's a helpful tip: If a fishmonger hands you a pint of crab meat or a side of fish that smells funny, request a replacement from the *front* of the refrigerated case. When refilling troughs of fish, seafood shops put the freshest fish near the front in order to sell the older product first.

Tips for buying fish

- Shop at a local independent fish market, if you can.
- Get to know your fishmonger.
- Ask him or her how to prepare different fish.
- Fresh fish looks moist and translucent. Older fish and fish that has been frozen look opaque.
- Smell before you buy. Fish should smell clean, neither fishy nor of ammonia.
- Even if a sign says "fresh," ask when it came in and when it was cut.
- "Fresh frozen" means it was fresh when frozen (well, we certainly *hope* so!).
- Buy wild whenever possible.
- Talk to your fishmonger about which species have higher mercury levels and try to avoid eating them too often.
- Buy smaller fish and more freshwater fish for lower mercury levels.
- Eating a wider variety of fish (as opposed to, for example, only tuna) can reduce your risk of mercury exposure.

Your sources

Know your store and, even better, the individuals you buy from. If you care enough to get to know the people who serve you, they will return the favor and make sure you are happy!

Over the years our vendors have become friends. Dominic at the cheese store goes the extra mile to fill a last-minute order, often throwing in a new product. Our favorite bagger makes sure to carefully place our fruit on top. Tony, the fishmonger, actually sings as he wraps our fish! All of these people make a trip to the market a great time.

We have been shopping at our local markets for more than fifteen years. It shows in the great service we receive and the great friends we've made doing so.

There are so many advantages to shopping at different markets! In Los Angeles, we are fortunate to have so many great specialty markets: the Greek market, the Italian deli, countless Mexican *carnicerías*, the French bakery and the Dutch deli. Then there are Japanese, Armenian, Persian, Hawaiian, Thai and Chinese markets. We know it isn't possible to find this kind of diversity everywhere, but if you take the time to explore your neighborhood more deeply, you will probably find something special there to inspire you!

Check our Resource section on pages 299–310 for online stores that sell most of the exotic spices and ingredients we love.

> Paper or plastic? Shopping every day adds up to a lot of shopping bags. We shop so much that, if we used paper, we wouldn't want to know how many trees that would add up to. Plastic bags are reusable (once), but most often not recyclable. As the Family Chef, you have the opportunity to do little things that make a big difference. Reusable bags are a smart idea. You can buy them online (we love reusablebags.com) and many grocery stores are now selling these bags at the checkout stand. If you keep them in your car they are an easy way to save time, money—and the planet!

We always remember how lucky we are to be Family Chefs because we don't have to prepare dishes on a set menu. And neither do you! Sometimes, Jill and I look at each other and say, "Wow, we *never* could have done that in a restaurant!" Like us, you can let the ebb and flow of fresh foods into your local markets and what's in season dictate what you prepare. We promise that if you do, your own family will wonder how you became such a genius with food.

tips for using this book

- Throughout the book, we have included many meals that contain the same ingredients. Using the same ingredients for multiple meals prevents waste and will save you time and money.
- Each recipe is set up to help you get all of your ingredients ready before you begin. We have written directions to help you prepare different elements simultaneously or in a particular order, for example, "While the fish is marinating, make the quinoa."
- Many of our recipes do not call for traditional measurements. We find that when shopping for ingredients, it is much easier if the recipe calls for one bunch of parsley, chopped, instead of trying to figure out how much parsley you would need for two tablespoons of chopped parsley. Feel free to experiment and adjust to your liking.
- When you sauté or grill fish, preheat your oven to 450 degrees F before you begin cooking. If the fish browns before it has cooked through, finish it for a few minutes in the oven. Restaurants use this technique all the time.
- When we call for citrus zest we find it's easier to use a microplane zester instead of a grater. Microplanes can be found at most cooking stores or even at some markets. This type of zester has very sharp blades and so you will only need to run it lightly over the fruit to remove the colored part of the skin. The white part underneath is bitter and should not be used.
- Always make sure the pan you cook with is very hot before you begin. You'll use less oil—because the heat disperses it quickly and evenly—and everything will cook better.
- If you read each recipe all the way through before you begin, your work will go more smoothly.
- As you cook and prepare these dishes, taste, taste, taste and season as you go. Even a marinade must taste good.

you have to eat in the morning

JILL SAYS • For a while, I was getting terrible headaches almost every day. Trying to figure out why, I realized I was cooking fresh, delicious breakfasts for everyone else at work and at home—but not for myself! The concept of starting the day off right with a good meal is not a new discovery. It's something I constantly emphasize to others. It was a big moment for me when I realized it was time to start loving and caring for myself in the same way I nurture the people around me. It's not that I don't like breakfast. In fact, I love it! I just needed to start remembering and acting like I did.

I can't tell you how many times a client says, "I just don't have time for breakfast." I used to make the mistake of asking people if they wanted something to eat in the morning. Now I just go ahead and make it. I've found that even people who claim they're not hungry in the morning usually eat breakfast when it materializes before them.

If they don't, I remind them that a lack of hunger in the morning is not a sign of health! We need to feed our metabolism early every day to get it moving.

We all know how important it is for kids to have a healthy breakfast. Since I'm a new mom, it's all the more vital for me to eat something healthy myself because my son, Charlie, watches me closely—and loves to eat off my plate.

But sometimes kids can be finicky. Our good friend Louise has a four-year-old son named Nicolas. One morning Nicolas decided that he had to have pizza for breakfast. Instead of saying no, Louise said, "Sure, how about pizza with scrambled eggs on it?" He loved it and they both got what they wanted. Try to keep an open mind and be creative when it comes to eating breakfast. It doesn't need to be the same thing every day.

you have to eat in the morning

no-excuse smoothies

JILL SAYS • We think smoothies are a great way to start the day. They're so easy to make that there's no excuse for *not* fueling up in the morning. Notice that, instead of fruit juice, we prefer coconut water (which is different from coconut milk) because it contains a lot less sugar. We also include milled flaxseed, which is an excellent source of omega-3.

We like to freeze our own fruit on sheet trays and then store it in freezer bags. We started doing this because the fruit at the farmers' market looks, smells and tastes so delicious that we tend to overbuy. An added bonus: Seasonal fruit from the farmers' market is usually so sweet that we don't add any sweetener. However, if you are not an overbuyer or don't have the time or the inclination to freeze your own fruit, frozen fruit from the market (try to find organic!) is perfectly acceptable.

SERVES 2.

white peach and ginger smoothie

$3/4$ cup plain yogurt (I prefer Greek yogurt)

2 cups frozen white (or yellow) peaches

$1/2$ teaspoon minced fresh ginger

1 tablespoon milled flaxseed

$1 1/2$ cups coconut water

1–2 tablespoons honey or agave nectar (optional)

tropical fruit smoothie

$3/4$ cup plain yogurt (I prefer Greek yogurt)

2 cups coconut water

2 cups tropical fruit (any mixture of pineapple, mango, papaya)

1 cup frozen bananas

$1/4$ cup passion fruit juice (optional)

1–2 tablespoons honey or agave nectar (optional)

berry smoothie

1 cup plain yogurt (I prefer Greek yogurt)

1¼ cups coconut water

2 cups frozen mixed berries

1 tablespoon milled flaxseed

1–2 tablespoons honey or agave nectar (optional)

Throw everything into the blender. Pour into a glass—and enjoy!

JILL'S SMART IDEA

Smoothies are a great after-school or anytime healthy snack for kids. Get your kids to pick their favorite fruits and divide them into freezer bags with their names on them.

don't waste food—make fried rice!

JILL SAYS • On weekends, my husband, Simon, gets up at the crack of dawn to catch the best waves. He loves it so much that he stays in the water for hours. By the time he gets home, he's always famished. He opens the fridge and, although it's almost full, doesn't find anything to eat. So, I get up to have a look myself and discover bits of leftovers from the past few days. Each little item by itself doesn't seem like enough, but I know I can throw it all together and there will be more than enough for both of us to enjoy! This recipe is a great way to use just about anything you have left over in the fridge.

SERVES 2–4.

2 tablespoons peanut oil or vegetable oil

1 egg, beaten

$1/2$ medium onion, diced, or 2–3 scallions, chopped (any kind of onion will work!)

1 teaspoon garlic, crushed, or sprinkle of garlic powder (optional)

1 teaspoon grated ginger (optional)

1 heaping cup veggies (This could be just broccoli or a mixture of whatever

veggies you have on hand, including asparagus, peppers, mushrooms, bean sprouts or green beans. Veggies can be cooked or raw.)

$1/2$–$3/4$ cups cooked meat, diced or shredded, such as chicken, pork or beef. You can even use leftover salmon.

2 cups cooked brown or white rice

salt and pepper and soy sauce, to taste

1. In a medium nonstick skillet, heat 1 teaspoon of oil and scramble egg until slightly dry. Set aside on a small plate.

2. In the same skillet, heat the remaining oil and add the onions, garlic and ginger. Sauté for 2–3 minutes. Now add the veggies and sauté for another 2–3 minutes. If they are raw, sauté for 5–6 minutes; if they are browning or too dry, add a tablespoon or two of water to create some steam to help them cook.

3. Add leftover meat and sauté another minute or so to reheat.

4. Add rice and cooked egg. Stir together and cook until warm. Season with salt and pepper to taste and a few dashes of soy, if you choose!

JEWELS' SMART IDEA

I use very, very small Frigoverre (page 302) food-storage containers made of glass to store even the smallest bits of food in the fridge—because I know I'll use them later. Part of being a good Family Chef is making your dollar and your food stretch!

turning japanese-style breakfast

JEWELS SAYS • Once when I was traveling with my clients and staying in a beautiful hotel. I decided I would try something different for breakfast. When room service arrived with this breakfast, I almost couldn't bear to eat it because it was so beautiful, sophisticated—and healthy! The warm, aromatic broth of the miso soup felt so comforting. The salmon was seasoned so simply that I could taste the deliciously subtle flavor of the fish. Little did I know as I savored it that morning that, one day, I would be re-creating it for my future husband (a man I had yet to meet), who is half-Japanese.

You can buy Japanese bento boxes at most Japanese markets or online. Of course you don't have to use one, but that's half the fun! You can be creative in all the different foods you use to fill the compartments. Here are some of the more traditional items:

BENTO BOX ELEMENTS
- miso soup (*So-Easy Miso Soup*, page 132)
- rice. I like red, black or short-grain sushi rice, but any will do.
- salmon. Heat the pan, use 1 glug of oil, salt and pepper and cook through.
- greens. Anything green (spinach, asparagus, kale, etc.)
- egg. Soft-boiled, poached or fried
- tea. Green tea is perfect!

JEWELS' SMART IDEA

You can make miso soup and, then, add the salmon, meat and veggies to the bowl for a delicious meal, anytime!

buenos días!
jill's favorite mexican breakfast

JILL SAYS • When we were growing up, our breakfasts often included beans, tortillas, chili and eggs in some form or another. I love any kind of Mexican breakfast that incorporates these ingredients—and I love, love, love a fried egg on anything! This is my take on some of my favorite things that our mom and nana used to make for us. I serve it all the time to my clients and my family, and everyone loves it. It gives me a thrill to serve the simple food I grew up on to people who appreciate it as much as I do—and come back for seconds and thirds.

SERVES 4–6.

> *Salsa* and *Guacamole* (recipes below)
> peanut oil (enough to fry tortillas)
> 6 corn tortillas
> 1½ cup cooked black beans or 1 15-ounce can, seasoned with salt,
>   cumin and garlic powder
> 6 eggs
> 1 cup grated cheese (I like a mixture of jack, cheddar and *cotija*)

1. Prepare the *Salsa* and *Guacamole*. Set aside.

2. The corn tortillas can be fried or baked. To fry, use a heavy skillet (cast-iron is best). Pour 1–1½ inches of peanut oil into the pan. If you fill the oil to the top of the pan, you won't have room during the frying for the oil to bubble up. Heat the oil to 375 degrees F. You really don't need a thermometer for this. You can just test the oil by putting a strip of tortilla in it. Once it sizzles and bubbles, the oil is hot enough. I fry one or two at a time until they are brown and crispy. Remove the tortilla and drain on a plate lined with paper towels. Salt them while they are still hot so the salt will stick to them. To bake the shells, set the oven to 350 F. Rub the tortillas with olive oil and sprinkle with salt. Place them on a sheet tray and bake for 10–15 minutes, until brown and crispy.

3. In a small pan, heat the beans and smash them up with a fork or potato masher. Keep warm on the stove while you fry or poach the eggs.

4. Divide the crispy tortillas onto 4–6 plates. Spread ¼ cup of beans on each tortilla. Add cheese, dividing evenly.

5. Place one egg on each tortilla. The heat from the eggs and beans will melt the cheese.

6. Top each one with a spoonful of salsa and guacamole. Enjoy!

salsa

MAKES 2 CUPS.

6 medium ripe tomatoes, cut up (Jewels likes to seed them and cut them into teeny, tiny pieces. I don't mind the seeds and don't have the time to cut them so small!)

¼ cup red onion, chopped

2 tablespoons cilantro, roughly chopped

1 serrano or jalapeño chili, finely chopped (can also roast, peel and chop)

½ teaspoon salt

¼ teaspoon garlic powder

Mix all of the ingredients in a bowl and let stand for a few minutes to allow the flavors to meld together. You can store this in the fridge for several days—I prefer to eat it at room temperature.

JILL'S SMART IDEA

Save your salsa and guacamole for a quick quesadilla, burrito *(Nana's Egg-and-Potato Burritos*, page 185; *Smart Idea Burritos*, page 187; *Mushroom Quesadillas on Whole-Wheat Tortillas*, page 189), scrambled eggs or ceviche *(Jewels' Cabo San Lucas Ceviche*, page 157).

guacamole

MAKES 3–4 CUPS.

4 large ripe (but not mushy) avocados (I love Haas!)

$1/4$ cup red onion, finely chopped

2 tablespoons cilantro, finely chopped

1 serrano or jalapeno chili, finely chopped

Juice of $1/2$ lime

$1/2$–1 teaspoon salt

$1/4$ teaspoon garlic powder or fresh minced garlic (optional)

1. Cut the avocados in half. Remove pit and use a spoon to scoop out flesh into a medium-sized bowl.

2. Add the remaining ingredients and mash with a fork or potato masher to achieve desired consistency. I like mine a little chunky.

To store guacamole in the fridge, place a piece of plastic wrap directly on top of the guacamole to protect it from air (which will turn it brown). Will keep for a couple of days in the fridge.

brekkie with your mates

JILL SAYS • One of my Australian husband Simon's favorite meals is a big breakfast (his other two favorites are lunch and dinner.) Aussies eat bacon and eggs, much as we do, but they add a few extras. I love this breakfast because it is hearty and includes veggies.

SERVES 2–4.

- 1 can of favorite baked beans
- 4 strips of bacon
- 12 brown or white mushrooms, rough end of stem removed
- 2 Roma tomatoes, cut in half
- 4 eggs
- 2 large handfuls of fresh spinach, roughly chopped
- salt and pepper

1. In a small pan, heat the beans and keep warm over a low flame while you prepare the rest of the meal.

2. In a large nonstick or cast-iron skillet, fry the bacon until crispy. Set aside and drain almost all of the grease from the pan.

3. In the same skillet, throw in the mushrooms and season with salt and pepper. In the other half of the skillet, place the tomatoes, skin side down, and cook for 2–3 minutes. Keep an eye on the mushrooms at the same time so they don't burn. Turn everything over and cook for another minute or so. Push the mushrooms and tomatoes to one side of the pan, and crack the eggs into the pan and fry. You may need to add a little bit of oil or bacon fat back into the pan to keep the eggs from sticking.

4. When the eggs are done, divide everything onto plates. Keep the pan on the stove and throw in the spinach to wilt (30 seconds to 1 minute) and add cooked spinach to plates.

5. Serve with baked beans and your favorite toast.

go greek for breakfast!

JILL SAYS • This is an easy way to make scrambled eggs taste as if they were prepared by a gourmet chef. Both versions of this recipe are great on-the-go morning meals. Kids especially like the burrito-style version.

eggs with feta cheese and parsley in pita

SERVES 4–6.

8 eggs

7 ounces feta cheese or goat cheese, crumbled

2 tablespoons chopped parsley

salt and pepper, to taste

1 tablespoon olive oil

4 pita bread rounds, cut in half

1 large handful of arugula or mixed greens

8 tablespoons *Tomato Chutney Spread* (page 191) or good store-bought tomato chutney

1. In a medium-sized mixing bowl, beat together the eggs, feta, parsley, and salt and pepper.

2. Heat a large nonstick skillet over medium heat. Add the olive oil and then the egg mixture. Cook until eggs are done.

3. Heat the pita in a toaster or toaster oven until slightly warm. Divide the egg mixture, arugula and tomato chutney evenly among the pita pockets.

baked burrito style

SERVES 4–6.

4 eggs

7 ounces feta cheese or goat cheese, crumbled

salt and pepper, to taste

2 tablespoons butter

2 tablespoons olive oil

6 10" flour tortillas

1. Preheat the oven to 350 F. In a small bowl, beat together the eggs, feta cheese and salt and pepper. In small pan, combine the butter and olive oil and melt butter. Set aside.

2. Brush a 9" × 13" sheet tray lightly with 1 tablespoon of the butter and oil mixture; save remainder for brushing on burritos.

3. Fill each tortilla with 4 tablespoons of raw egg and feta mixture, fold in the sides and roll up like a burrito. Place on prepared tray.

4. Brush the outside of each burrito with the remaining butter and oil mixture. Bake for 35–40 minutes, or until the burritos are golden and crispy.

JILL'S SMART IDEA

These crispy treats can be made ahead of time, stored in the fridge in an airtight container and reheated in the oven or toaster oven for just a few minutes.

the absolute best healthy granola

JILL SAYS • I love crunchy granola. I think it is great for breakfast or for a snack. Sometimes I put it on cottage cheese to give it crunch. I also love dry fruit (especially raisins) in my granola. But, in order to keep the granola crunchy, I have found it's best to add the dry fruit just before eating it. This recipe is inspired by one created by a Family Chef named Elaine. After she was generous enough to share it with me, I added variations of my own. It's so simple that I make it all the time and give lots away to family and friends.

MAKES 10–15 SERVINGS.

5 cups rolled thick oats

$1/2$ cup wheat germ

$1/2$ cup whole-wheat flour

$1/2$ cup milled flaxseed

$1/2$ cup sesame seeds

2 cups whole almonds

2 cups whole pecans

$1/2$ teaspoon sea salt

$3/4$ cup grapeseed oil or extra-light olive oil

$3/4$ cup honey (I like Greek honey, if you can find it)

1. Preheat the oven to 325 degrees F. Line two large sheet trays with parchment paper or Silpat (a nonstick silicone mat you can cook on).

2. In a large mixing bowl, stir together all of the dry ingredients.

3. Heat the oil and honey in a small saucepan over medium-low heat until the honey is warm and runny.

4. Stir the oil and honey mixture into the dry ingredients with a wooden spoon.

5. Divide mixture evenly between the two sheet trays, spreading it out as evenly as possible.

6. Bake for 35–45 minutes, stirring occasionally so the edges don't brown too much. Remove from the oven and let cool on sheet trays. Store in airtight containers in your pantry.

JILL'S SMART IDEA

Sprinkle granola on oatmeal in the morning or eat with yogurt and fruit for breakfast. You can also snack on it throughout the day.

something different on toast— try it, you'll like it!

JILL SAYS • Like everyone else, I am often in a hurry and *think* I don't have time for breakfast in the morning. Because I get low blood sugar, which can cause terrible headaches, I simply must eat. I have found that low-fat cottage cheese is an excellent source of protein that you can eat on the run, if necessary. The apple butter lends just a touch of sweetness and the granola adds crunch (because I love crunch!).

SERVES 2–4.

    4 slices whole-wheat bread
    4 tablespoons favorite apple butter (try to get one with little to no sugar)
    1 cup low-fat cottage cheese
    $1/2$–$3/4$ cup The Absolute Best Healthy Granola (page 69)

Toast bread. Top each slice with one tablespoon apple butter, $1/4$ cup cottage cheese and a generous sprinkle of granola.

a salad a day keeps the pounds away

JEWELS SAYS • Salad is more than just lettuce. It can be fresh parsley with chunks of beautiful ripe tomatoes or thinly sliced celery combined with salty and savory pecorino cheese. The recipes in this section are designed to help you think outside the box when you make a salad. They feature fruit, beans, cucumbers, artichokes and grilled mushrooms. I keep tiny little glass food-storage containers of tasty bits and pieces of leftovers that might not look like much but, when used in a salad, can provide the perfect means of using that small piece of leftover chicken or steak from the night before.

The secret to a *great* salad is to make each and every element count. Season each ingredient before you put it on the plate or in the bowl to toss. Then think about how you can add texture to your salad. Even chopping the exact same items differently than you did the day before will create a new dish! Don't forget to "dress a salad," even if you just use fresh lemon juice and fruity extra-virgin olive oil. Making a fresh dressing can be the difference between a good salad and a great salad, so we've also included a few variations on a classic vinaigrette for you to experiment with.

Eating one meal a day full of leafy greens is the perfect way to keep yourself slim and trim. Once you have eaten a tasty, well-balanced salad made from fantastically fresh produce, you will begin to see salad as something you and your family can have for more than just the obligatory first course—as a full, satisfying meal filled with amazing flavors and textures.

a salad a day keeps the pounds away

the formula for salad dressing (9 kinds!)

JEWELS SAYS • The difference between a salad made with a bottled dressing and a fresh dressing is immense. It is so easy to take a salad to its full potential! Experiment with different acids and oil and you can turn "just a salad" into a tasty meal!

There are so many ways to make a dressing. When I am tailoring a dressing to a particular salad, this is the formula I follow:

1. choose an acid

   citrus juice
   (for example lemon, lime, grapefruit or orange)
   vinegar (there are so many to choose from)

2. adjust the acidity

   with a little salt and/or sugar

3. choose an oil

   some good choices are olive oil, grapeseed oil or sunflower oil

4. add a base flavor

   shallots or garlic

5. you can add

   herbs (dill, marjoram, oregano)
   fruit
   veggies
   nuts (any will do)

6. bind it together with

   Dijon mustard
   garlic
   egg yolk

7. and finally . . .

   shake it, whisk it, stir it or blend it!

JEWELS' SMART IDEA

Salad dressings generally last a week. So, every time you make one, make enough for the week!

a lovely little dressing!
JEWELS SAYS

MAKES 3/4 CUP.

- 1/4 cup sherry vinegar (I use agretto di vino santo di montevertine)
- 1/2 shallot, minced
- 1/2 teaspoon sugar
- 1/2 teaspoon salt
- 1/2 teaspoon Dijon mustard
- 1/4 teaspoon fresh marjoram and/or oregano, minced
- 1/2 cup extra-virgin olive oil (I use olio extra vergine di oliva di montevertine)

Mix it up with a whisk or double the recipe and put it in the blender.

grilled-tomato vinaigrette
JEWELS SAYS

MAKES 1 CUP.

- 1/2 lime, juiced
- a pinch sugar
- a pinch salt
- 1/2 cup *Grilled-Tomato Puree* (page 119)
- 1/2 shallot, minced
- 1 tablespoon Dijon mustard
- 1/2 cup olive oil

1. Put the first three ingredients in a jar or in a bowl and mix.

2. Add the remaining ingredients and mix.

avocado makes you a goddess dressing
JEWELS SAYS

MAKES 3/4 CUP.

- a pinch sugar
- a few pinches salt
- 1/2 lime, juiced
- 1 whole avocado
- 1/2 shallot
- 1/2 tablespoon Dijon mustard
- 1/2 cup extra-virgin olive oil

1. Blend first three ingredients in a blender.

2. Add the remaining ingredients and blend. If you need more liquid you can add a bit of ice water.

tahini dressing
JEWELS SAYS

MAKES 1 CUP.

$^1/_2$ shallot, minced

$^1/_2$ clove garlic, minced

1 teaspoon parsley, minced

$^1/_2$ cup tahini paste

$^1/_2$ cup extra-virgin olive oil

$^1/_2$ cup warm water

Mix all ingredients in a bowl with a fork or shake in a glass jar.

pomegranate vinaigrette
JILL SAYS

MAKES 1 CUP.

2 tablespoons pomegranate concentrate or $^1/_2$ cup pomegranate juice reduced down over a low flame to 2 tablespoons

2 tablespoons champagne wine vinegar (you can also use white or red wine vinegar)

2 tablespoons finely chopped shallot (approximately 1 small shallot)

$^1/_2$ teaspoon salt

$^3/_4$ cup extra-virgin olive oil

1. In a small bowl put pomegranate concentrate, vinegar, shallots and salt.

2. Mix with a whisk and let sit for a few minutes to dissolve the salt.

3. Slowly whisk in the olive oil.

4. Taste and add pepper and more salt if desired.

asian dressing
JEWELS SAYS

MAKES ¾ CUP.

¼ cup regular or brown rice vinegar

⅓ cup roasted sesame oil

a pinch sugar

a pinch salt

¼ shallot, minced

3 tablespoons soy sauce

a pinch raw sesame seeds

Mix all ingredients together.

cara cara vinaigrette
JEWELS SAYS

MAKES ½ CUP.

juice from ½ cara cara orange

½ shallot, minced

½ teaspoon Dijon mustard

a pinch salt

¼ cup grapeseed oil

(you can also add dill, chives or chive
  flowers)

Mix all ingredients together.

mexican caesar dressing
JILL SAYS

MAKES 1 CUP.

1/4 cup lemon juice

1 teaspoon red wine vinegar

2 tablespoons anchovy paste

1 tablespoon Worcestershire sauce

1 small garlic clove, minced

1 teaspoon cumin seeds, toasted

1 teaspoon ancho chili powder

1 tablespoon cilantro, roughly chopped

3/4 cup extra-virgin olive oil

1/2 cup good-quality Parmesan cheese, grated

salt and pepper, to taste

Put all of the ingredients in a blender and turn on for a minute, just until well combined.

lemon truffle vinaigrette
JILL SAYS

MAKES 3/4 CUP.

3 tablespoons lemon juice

2 tablespoons shallot, finely chopped (approximately 1 small shallot)

1/2 teaspoon salt

1/4 cup good-quality Parmesan cheese, grated (I use a microplaner)

1 tablespoon truffle oil

1/2 cup extra-virgin olive oil

1/4 teaspoon fresh ground pepper

1. Place lemon juice, shallots and salt in a small mixing bowl. Let sit a few minutes to dissolve the salt.

2. Add Parmesan cheese.

3. Slowly whisk in oils.

4. Taste and season with more pepper and salt, if desired.

delicious, clean and healthy tostada

JEWELS SAYS • I live in Southern California, where Mexican cuisine is very popular and, typically, pretty heavy. But Mexican food can be light, delicious and very flavorful if you combine the right ingredients. This is a very healthy salad if you are trying to mix it up while slimming down!

The achiote marinade is a big winner, so track down the achiote paste, if possible. Achiote paste, usually found in Mexican markets, is made from ground annatto seeds. This marinade keeps for quite a while and tastes great on meat or fish as well. I love to use boneless, skinless chicken thighs for more flavor.

SERVES 4–6.

THE TORTILLA SHELLS

> **6 corn tortillas, one for each tostada**
>
> **1/8 cup oil**

THE BEANS

> **1 cup black beans (fresh cooked or canned)**
>
> **1 serrano or jalapeño chili, minced**
>
> **1 lime, juiced**
>
> **1 tablespoon ground cumin**
>
> **1/2 tablespoon chili powder**
>
> **1/4 teaspoon garlic powder**
>
> **2 shakes Tapatío Hot Sauce (or any hot sauce)**

THE SALAD

> **1/4 head cabbage**
>
> **1/4 head lettuce**
>
> **1 bunch cilantro leaves, coarsely chopped**
>
> **2 spring green onions, thinly sliced**
>
> **2 tomatoes, seeded and thinly sliced**
>
> **1/3 cup *cotija* cheese**
>
> **1 avocado, sliced**
>
> **1/4 cup *Pickled Red Onion* (recipe below)**
>
> **(You can use the *Grilled-Tomato Vinaigrette* [page 78] on this salad.)**

THE CHICKEN

> **2 whole chicken breasts (or 4 half chicken breasts)**
>
> ***Achiote Marinade* (recipe below)**

1. Prepare the *Achiote Marinade*.

2. Marinate chicken for at least 20 minutes (and as long as overnight).

3. While the chicken is marinating, prepare the *Pickled Red Onion*.

4. Brush tortillas lightly with oil and bake at about 350 degrees F until crispy.

5. Toss beans with serrano chilis, cumin, chili powder, garlic powder, salt and hot sauce, to taste.

6. Grill the chicken, cool slightly and slice thinly.

7. Toss all salad ingredients with a little juice from the pickled red onion and some olive oil or toss with the *Grilled-Tomato Vinaigrette*.

8. Assemble the tostadas: Pile the beans and thinly sliced chicken on the crispy tortillas shells; then add the salad.

pickled red onion

MAKES 2 CUPS.

    1 red onion, thinly sliced
    $^3/_4$ cup vinegar (unseasoned rice, coconut or champagne)
    $^1/_4$ cup kosher salt
    $^1/_4$ cup sugar

Mix everything together and let sit until desired taste and texture is achieved, 10 minutes to overnight.

achiote marinade

MAKES 1 CUP.

    $^1/_4$ cup achiote paste
    1 clove garlic
    2 teaspoons salt
    1 teaspoon cumin
    $^1/_2$ cup light oil (can be a mixture of safflower and peanut)
    1 lime, juiced (if marinating overnight, use to coat chicken or meat or fish just before grilling)

Mix everything up in a blender and taste. Should be slightly salty.

JILL'S SMART IDEA

Make extra achiote marinade to use for the *Achiote-Marinated Pork Tenderloin* (page 217) or to marinate chicken, fish or lamb.

to chop salad—jewels' version

JEWELS SAYS • The head chef in the catering kitchen where I first worked used to demonstrate cutting an onion for me and then give me a huge sack of onions (so heavy I could not lift it alone) and tell me to get started. When I was more than halfway through the bag—sometimes hours later—he would check on my work and compare my pieces to his example. If they were not precisely the same size, he would throw a huge "chef tantrum," toss everything I'd chopped into the garbage and holler for someone to bring me another sack of onions so I could begin again. Despite that experience, I now find chopping so calming and therapeutic that I look forward to working at my cutting board. Once you feel truly confident about doing something you can begin to enjoy it. With a sharp knife and a little practice, I hope you will enjoy chopping this salad up, too!

SERVES 4–6.

2 heads curly red-leaf lettuce

a handful of fresh parsley

4 small Persian cucumbers (or one English cucumber)

4 Roma or other small ripe tomatoes

¼ red onion

1 bunch asparagus, blanched

½ cup good-quality Parmesan or pecorino Romano cheese, shaved

1. Wash the lettuce and parsley. Chop finely.

2. Peel, seed and finely dice cucumbers.

3. Seed tomatoes and dice them along with the onions.

4. Blanch asparagus in boiling water for one minute; then place in a bowl of ice water until completely cool. Dry completely and finely dice.

5. Toss together in a large bowl with cheese and dressing of your choice.

Try this with *Pomegranate Vinaigrette* (page 79), *Grilled-Tomato Vinaigrette*, (page 78), or just a few glugs of good-quality extra-virgin olive oil and a couple of splashes of vinegar.

or not to chop salad—jill's version

using the same ingredients as Jewels' version.

Salad is really so easy to make. Be sure to use super-fresh ingredients to make the simplest salad simply delicious!

SERVES 4–6.

1. Wash lettuce and tear into large pieces.

2. Peel cucumbers and slice into rounds.

3. Cut tomatoes in large chunky pieces.

4. Cut red onion into thin strips.

5. Cut asparagus in half. Blanch in boiling water for one minute; then place in a bowl of ice water to cool. Dry completely.

6. Tear parsley into pieces.

Toss it all together in a large salad bowl with cheese and dressing of your choice. Fast, easy, fresh and yummy!

Try this with *Pomegranate Vinaigrette* (page 79), *Grilled-Tomato Vinaigrette* (page 78) or just a few glugs of good-quality extra-virgin olive oil and a couple of splashes of vinegar.

"It's difficult to think anything but pleasant thoughts while eating a homegrown tomato."

—Lewis Grizzard

halloumi cheese with cucumber lentil salad

JILL SAYS • In my travels to Australia, I often noticed this delicious cheese on menus. I had never heard of it before, so I thought I would give it a try and I'm so glad I did—I loved it! Back home, I started to look for it and was pleasantly surprised to find it in my local grocery market, as well as my favorite Italian deli, which is chock-full of great cheeses. This cheese is a little on the salty side, so it's marvelous with the cool, fresh taste of cucumber and lemon.

SERVES 2–4.

 6 Persian cucumbers, peeled in strips and cut into half-circles
 4 ripe tomatoes (Japanese if you can find them), cut in big chunks
 2 tablespoons parsley, chopped
 1 teaspoon mint, chopped
 1 cup cooked beluga or Puy lentils (I prefer beluga)
 3 tablespoons extra-virgin olive oil
 $1/2$ lemon, juiced
 salt and pepper
 1–2 glugs extra-virgin olive oil
 1 7-ounce package halloumi cheese, sliced into 12 pieces

1. Place the first seven ingredients in a bowl and toss together.

2. Season lightly with salt and pepper. Do not oversalt because the cheese is salty enough.

3. Heat a large nonstick skillet over medium-high heat and add a splash or two of oil.

4. Place the halloumi cheese in pan and sauté for 1-2 minutes, just until golden.

5. Turn cheese over and brown for another minute.

6. Remove from pan and serve immediately, while cheese is still warm, with cucumber lentil salad.

JILL'S SMART IDEA

You can also use fresh cooked or canned beans (any kind) or quinoa in the place of lentils. The halloumi cheese is also wonderful with Jewels' version of *Chickpea Salad* (page 278).

seared tuna sashimi salad—
the ultimate skinny

JEWELS SAYS • This salad is inspired by Chef Nobu Matsuhisa. I have been a huge fan of his since I first began cooking. To me, he represents perfect balance. He combines the dignity and precision of traditional Japanese cuisine with "fashion-forward" innovations tailored to his Western audience.

No matter how much I raved to my boss about the wonderful world of raw fish, she remained unconvinced until we decided to visit the chef's restaurant, Matsuhisa, together. As we took our seats, I conveyed real confidence that we would find something she would like (note: If *you* like what you make or what you are eating, your friends and guests will trust you!). I ordered the Seared Sashimi Salad—and it was a huge hit! Hooray! That one meal expanded our culinary horizon—which is fun for chef and diner alike!

Seared sashimi and greens is a great combination for anyone who wants to eat light and still have the energy to make it through a busy day. There are a lot of ways to make this pretty-looking salad, so improvise! Also, keep in mind that the key is the dressing. Chef Matsuhisa recommends cutting the onions and then rinsing them to remove the sharpness. I have also added cucumber for texture and lightness.

SERVES 2.

the salad

ANY SPICY GREENS WILL DO BUT THIS IS A GREAT COMBINATION:

3 handfuls Napa cabbage, sliced thin

2 handfuls tatsoi

2 stalks celery, thinly sliced on a diagonal

2 scallions, thinly sliced on a diagonal

1 handful cilantro leaves

1 carrot, julienned

1/2 handful daikon, very thinly sliced

2 myogas (ginger buds), super-thinly sliced

1/2 handful mitsuva (Japanese parsley)

1 shiso leaf (perilla), sliced thin

Put all of this in a bowl and cover with a damp paper towel and put in the fridge until you are ready to serve.

the dressing

2 tablespoons brown rice vinegar

½ teaspoon sugar

½ teaspoon salt

1 small onion, finely chopped (can be
   in processor) and rinsed under cold
   water

1 small Persian or Japanese cucumber

2 tablespoons soy sauce

1 tablespoon wasabi or dry mustard

1 tablespoon Asian sesame seed oil

¼ cup grapeseed oil, safflower oil or
   light olive oil

1. Mix the vinegar, sugar and salt.

2. In a processor or blender, add the remainder of the ingredients and pulse until blended (don't overblend—you still want to see small chunks of onion and cucumber).

3. I like to put this back in the fridge to keep it really cold until I make the salad.

the tuna

black sesame seeds

salt and pepper

a glug of extra-virgin olive oil

1 8-ounce piece of ahi tuna

1. Sprinkle the sesame seeds and salt and pepper over the tuna.

2. Press into the raw tuna until it sticks. Do this on all sides.

3. Heat a pan over medium-high heat until hot (about a minute) and then add a little glug of oil. Once the oil is hot, add the tuna and sear for about 45 seconds on each side.

4. Let cool for a moment and slice.

5. Put it all together: Toss the greens with a little oil, salt and pepper and arrange on a plate. Pour a little dressing next to it and place the tuna on top of the dressing.

JEWELS' SMART IDEA

Make the greens, dressing and ahi tuna ahead of time and you will be able to spend time with your company after they arrive! This is also a nice salad to take with you; just be sure to have a little ice pack for the tuna.

parsley is the key to success salad

JEWELS SAYS • When Jill and I were teenagers, one of our first jobs was working for an Armenian caterer. Jill's best friend, Karrie, who also became a professional Family Chef, got us the jobs so that we could all make extra money—and get out of the house. Though hired as waitresses, we all found ourselves drawn to the kitchen. We were fascinated by the tradition of the mezza platter, an array of many small appetizer plates served before a meal. One of the greatest discoveries we made was tabouleh, which is essentially a parsley salad. Parsley contains vitamin A, beta-carotene, vitamin C, folic acid and so much more. It is an amazing food—and so fresh-tasting it even freshens your breath!

SERVES 4–6.

2 bunches of curly parsley, chopped small

1 bunch Italian flat leaf parsley, chopped small

1/2 bunch fresh mint leaves, chopped small

2–3 green onions, chopped small

4 Persian cucumbers (or any other kind), chopped small

4 Roma tomatoes (or any other kind), seeded and chopped small

1/2–3/4 cup beluga lentils or quinoa

a few glugs extra-virgin olive oil

1 lemon, juiced

raw cauliflower, chopped really small (optional)

about 1/2 cup or more feta cheese (we prefer French feta [optional])

grilled shrimp (optional)

Put it all in a bowl and mix. Season and eat!

JEWELS' SMART IDEA

ou can also use a food processor to make quick work of all the chopping!

you don't need the barbecue to grill it salad

JEWELS SAYS • I've been known to grill in the most absurd places because, whatever the weather, it's simply one of the best ways to prepare lean and tasty food. I have grilled in 15-degree-below temperatures in the snow. In a pinch, I have fashioned a grill out of wood and coat hangers while on location with clients. Don't try this at home unless you want people to think you are eccentric! You can get some of the same barbecue effect, without a barbecue, by "pan grilling" indoors. Even if you don't have a special grill pan (one that makes grill marks), you can simply use a very hot pan, or a very hot broiler, on a stove top.

The warm, "grilled" ingredients in this dish paired with the cool, crunchy celery and tender mâche lettuce make for a delectable combination. If you can, use porcinis that are so ripe that their gills have a slight green tinge to them. Be sure to cook them really well. If porcinis aren't in season, you can also use brown, shitake, oyster or chanterelle mushrooms.

SERVES 2–4.

½ cup *Jewels' Grill Marinade* (recipe below)

3–4 large fresh porcini mushrooms, cut in quarters

1 bunch asparagus, thin or cut in half lengthwise

3 handfuls mâche lettuce or butter or red-leaf lettuce

3–4 red Belgian endives, torn into large pieces (can be white)

2 stalks celery, sliced medium-thin

1 dozen yellow baby tomatoes (I prefer yellow, but any color will do)

a few tablespoons *A Lovely Little Dressing* (page 78)

salt and pepper

1 dozen long thinly shaved slices of good-quality Parmesan

1. Prepare *Jewels' Grill Marinade*. Pour ½ cup of the marinade in a bowl and mix gently with the mushrooms and asparagus. Let sit for a bit.

2. "Grill" the veggies over high heat, beginning with the mushrooms as they take the longest. The asparagus stalks should retain their shape and stay green. After cooking, put the veggies back into whatever marinade you have left over and toss to coat.

3. Mix the mâche, Belgian endive and celery with a bit of dressing, salt and pepper and divide onto plates.

4. Add the grilled veggies and tomatoes, and top with shaved Parmesan.

jewels' grill marinade

You can use almost any combination of these herbs to make a tasty grill marinade. Remember that when you are using strong herbs like rosemary you can use a little less. For this reason I prefer using savory and thyme. This marinade keeps well so, once made, you can store some in a jar in the fridge. I use it mainly to marinate both veggies and chicken before grilling.

MAKES 1 CUP.

    1 clove of garlic, roughly chopped

    2 shallots, roughly chopped

    1/2 handful fresh thyme leaves, roughly chopped

    a big pinch of fresh savory and

    a big pinch of fresh rosemary leaves, roughly chopped

    2 leaves of fresh sage, chopped fine

    a big pinch of fresh marjoram, chopped fine

    zest of one lemon, chopped

    a pinch of crushed red pepper

    the following can be adjusted for strength (more oil and vinegar will make a milder marinade):

        about 1/4 cup of balsamic vinegar

        about 3/4 cup of extra-virgin olive oil

    plenty of salt and pepper, to taste

Mix everything together. Taste and adjust spices.

"Live, love, eat."

—Wolfgang Puck

hydrate with a fruity salad

JEWELS SAYS • Surprise! This is an easy one from me! I like to make it when cara cara oranges are in season. They have an unusual acid balance that works well with the cheese. Speaking of cheese, this recipe calls for *cotija* cheese. This is a Mexican cheese that is now found in a lot of supermarkets. If you can't find it, just use a crumbly cheese. Even bleu cheese will do.

SERVES 2–4.

- 1/4 cup *pepitas* (Mexican pumpkin seeds)
- 2 oranges (peel and slice, saving any juices)
- *Cara Cara Vinaigrette* (page 80)
- 1 head Grenoble or Parella lettuce (or any red-leaf lettuce)
- 3 handfuls mache lettuce
- a few *Pickled Red Onions* (page 85)
- 1/2 handful *cotija* cheese, crumbled or grated

1. Toast the *pepitas* on a sheet tray in the oven or in a dry skillet on the stove. Don't toast them too much or they will become tough and chewy. We want them to crunch!

2. Make the *Cara Cara Vinaigrette* using the reserved orange juice.

3. Mix all the lettuce and *Pickled Red Onions* together, and toss lightly with a little dressing. Top with the orange slices. Crumble the cheese over all and sprinkle a few seeds on top.

arugula, shaved artichoke and toasted hazelnut salad

JILL SAYS • As with many people, there was a time when I didn't know what to do with artichokes, especially the little ones. I wondered how to clean and prepare them. I've since discovered that, once you've cleaned a few artichokes, you will see how easy it really is to do. So don't be afraid and give it a try! I have found so many great ways to prepare and eat artichokes and this is one of my very favorites. After having fresh, finely shaved artichokes at an Italian restaurant, I was inspired to make this salad. My *Lemon Truffle Vinaigrette* (page 81) really puts it over the top. But it also tastes great with nothing more than extra-virgin olive oil and a little drizzled lemon juice.

SERVES 4–6.

Lemon Truffle Vinaigrette (page 81)

1/2 **lemon**

8 **baby artichokes**

6 **big handfuls of baby arugula**

1/2 **cup toasted hazelnuts, roughly chopped (toast at 350 degrees F for 8–10 minutes)**

a handful of parsley, roughly chopped (optional)

1/2 **cup good-quality Pecorino Romano cheese or good-quality Parmesan, shaved**

salt and pepper, to taste

1. Prepare the *Lemon Truffle Vinaigrette*. Set aside.

2. Prepare the artichokes: Keep the 1/2 lemon nearby. Cut off the tops of the artichokes and tear off all of the outer leaves until you get to the soft yellow inner leaves. Working quickly so they do not turn brown, rub with the lemon half as you go. At this point you can keep the artichokes in a bowl of cold lemon water until you are ready to cut them.

3. Just before serving the salad, cut the artichokes in half and see if you need to remove the choke, the hairy, silky white material just above the heart. You can do so with a small spoon or knife. The choke can be prickly and is usually removed in restaurants. If the artichoke is small enough, it will be tender and barely visible and you can leave it.

4. Slice the artichokes into very thin slices, place in a bowl with 2 tablespoons of the vinaigrette and toss together (I do this because the oil and lemon will keep the artichokes from turning brown too quickly).

5. In a large salad bowl, place the arugula, hazelnuts, parsley (if using) and most of the cheese.

6. Toss together with the artichokes and just a bit more dressing. It won't need a lot more dressing, as there is already dressing on the artichokes and you don't want to drown your arugula.

7. Season with salt and pepper and top with the remainder of the cheese.

JILL'S SMART IDEA

Instead of the artichokes, try crispy, julienned Fuji apples and a few slices of prosciutto on the side!

super-easy white bean salad

JEWELS SAYS • This is a satisfying but light salad. I like it with tons of fresh herbs, but you can also make it with dried oregano, dill and parsley, too. The key to this is to taste and season with salt, pepper, oil and vinegar. This salad can stand on its own or serve as a fantastic accompaniment to grilled chicken, meat or fish!

SERVES 2–4.

    2 cups cooked white beans, rinsed and drained
    1 cup cucumber, diced (can peel and seed)
    $1/2$ bulb fennel, super-thinly sliced
    2 fresh tomatoes, diced (including juices)
    3 stalks celery, diced
    1 bunch Italian flat-leaf parsley, rough chopped
    1 bunch chives or 2 green onions, chopped
    $1/2$ bunch dill and/or chervil
    a few celery leaves (use the inside white tender leaves)
    $1/2$ lemon squeezed over the top
    a few glugs extra-virgin olive oil
    a few glugs good sherry wine vinegar
    salt and pepper, to taste

1. Put it all in a bowl.

2. Taste and season.

JILL'S SMART IDEA

Jewels insists on using freshly cooked beans for this recipe, but I think it's just as delicious with beans straight out of a can!

soup can change your life

JEWELS SAYS • On September 11, 2001, I went to work in a fog. That day, I was working as a Family Chef for high-tech entrepreneur Lee Perlman's family. The Perlmans have strong ties to New York City. They were pretty quiet when I arrived. Clustered around the television, they waited to hear from relatives from the city who hadn't been able to get calls out. The thought of making fancy food that day didn't feel right. I took out some tomatoes and began slicing.

I have a thing about tomatoes. I like to keep a good store of them in my kitchen. I can find a use for them every day (Jill can, too). That day, I made the best basic tomato soup I could and toasted up some grilled cheese sandwiches to go along with it.

Everyone moved from the TV to the table as I put out the food. Slowly they started talking and connecting with one another. They asked for seconds and thirds. It wasn't the "chefiest" meal I've ever made, but I felt like I gave them exactly what they needed.

That's the magic of soup. It has the power to comfort, nourish and give you strength. Something bonding happens when everyone shares a good soup out of the same pot.

Once you are comfortable making soup you will realize that you can make it out of almost anything, including leftovers. The possibilities are endless. On Sunday, I like to make a little extra food for my house, so that we can have it during our busy week. It is really my favorite day to make soups! I love having soup on hand so that I can offer something delicious to friends and neighbors who stop by. When I've finished stirring and simmering, I like to pour the finished product into glass jars and store them in the fridge. I take secret pleasure in peeking inside to admire my soups before they disappear.

You will find that some of the soups in this section contain staples from meals from other chapters. The meatballs in the *Beautiful, Clean Albondigas Soup* (page 125), for instance, are made with the same ingredients as *Turkey Patties for Manly Men* (page 177). The *Wonton Soup* (page 127) uses the same recipe as the *Chicken Potstickers* (page 237). As you may have noticed, lentils are our secret weapon. So, of course, we've included lentil soup—one version from Jewels and one from Jill.

We love to experiment with different spices in our soups. Jill gave me a great strategy for doing so. When you want to see how a new ingredient, like truffle salt, flavors a soup, spoon a little soup into a cup and add the tiniest pinch of the new ingredient. Then taste. If it's good, you know it's safe to add to the whole pot!

soup can change your life

cool, cleansing celery soup— jewels' version

JEWELS SAYS • This is my favorite cold soup because it's satisfying and slimming. I dreamed it up when I needed something that sticks to your ribs, but processes easily through the body to help Jill and me execute our ongoing feel-good-in-a-bikini plan. I am a huge fan of the benefits of parsley, so, at the end, I use tons to add vitamins and beautiful color.

SERVES 6–8.

extra-virgin olive oil

1 onion, cut in medium pieces

1 leek, whites only (optional)

$1/2$ fennel bulb (optional, but I think fennel makes this soup deliciously unusual; I use fennel almost every day in something)

6 cups ($1^1/2$ boxes) chicken stock

1 potato, cut into medium pieces (You can also use cooked white beans or even rice!)

salt and pepper

12 stalks of celery, cut in medium chunks

1 bunch Italian flat-leaf parsley

2 handfuls of frozen peas

a pinch of nutmeg, cayenne and/or white pepper

salt, to taste

This soup can be served hot or cold. If cold, prepare a refrigerated bowl or fill a pot with ice water to strain the soup into; this helps to cool the soup quickly and retain its beautiful bright green color.

1. Heat a dry pan on the stove top. Once warm, add a splash of olive oil or butter and throw in the onions, leeks and fennel. Stir to release flavor. Do not brown.

2. Quickly add chicken stock and potatoes. Season with salt and pepper. Cook until potatoes are tender.

3. Add celery and cover. Cook just until tender.

4. If serving cold, fill a large bowl with ice and rest another empty bowl on top of ice.

5. In about two batches, put the soup in the blender. Add a handful of parsley and a handful of peas to each. Blend well.

6. If serving cold, pour pureed soup through a fine-mesh strainer into the bowl resting on the ice. Push through quickly so it can cool!

7. If serving hot, strain the pureed soup through a fine-mesh strainer into a pot and reheat until warmed through.

8. Adjust the salt and season with a pinch of nutmeg, cayenne pepper and/or white pepper. Enjoy!

JEWELS' SMART IDEA

Add red quinoa for protein to make a complete meal; the quinoa adds great texture, especially when served cold! When the soup is cold, we've also discovered we can actually drink it for a meal on the run. One of Jewels' clients loves to sip this throughout the day to satisfy her appetite. We also think it's chic with a little bit of white truffle oil and chives on top.

so-easy celery soup—jill's version

JILL SAYS • I love Jewels' celery soup, but it's a little time-consuming. This is my so-easy version for celery soup. As with many of my soups, I use cauliflower for flavor and a creamy texture.

SERVES 6–8.

- 4 cups celery, chopped in 1" pieces (approximately 8 ribs)
- 1/2 head cauliflower, cut into 2" pieces (or one potato, peeled and cut)
- 1 small onion, cut into 1" pieces
- 8 cups chicken broth (I like Shelton's organic) or vegetable stock
- 1/2 teaspoon salt
- 1 tablespoon heavy cream (optional)

1. Put all ingredients, except the cream, in a large stockpot.

2. Bring to a boil, reduce to simmer and skim any impurities off the top.

3. Simmer for 20–30 minutes until vegetables are tender.

4. Blend (with hand blender or in blender) and stir in cream, if desired.

5. If you pureed the soup in a blender, return the soup to the pot and gently reheat if necessary. Taste and adjust seasoning with salt and pepper, if necessary. Easy and delicious!

JILL'S SMART IDEA

You can also use cooked white beans or cooked rice to add some thickness if you don't have cauliflower.

better than jill's lentil soup

JEWELS SAYS • One day I wanted to make lentil soup a little differently, using red lentils (sometimes called pink or crimson) instead of green or brown—and I wanted to give it an Indian flair for my client who didn't *think* she loved Indian food. On my quest to expand her culinary palate, I started out with a lot of "great ideas," but once this soup was under way, I got stuck. It turned out OK, but not great. I had just a bit of leftover *A Different Color Tomato Soup* (page 121) I had made the day before. It was the secret ingredient!

SERVES 6–8.

2 glugs olive oil

1 onion, diced

1/2 teaspoon garlic, minced

1/2 teaspoon ginger, minced

1/2 fennel bulb, diced

2 shallots, diced

2–5 threads saffron

2 pinches turmeric

3 big pinches ground coriander

3 cups chicken stock

3 cups cooked red lentils

1 cup *A Different Color Tomato Soup* (page 121)

salt, to taste

1. Heat a dry pot over a medium flame. When warm, add the olive oil, onion, ginger, garlic, fennel, shallots, saffron, turmeric and coriander. Sauté for a few minutes, until aromatic. Do not overdo or the spices will burn.

2. Pour in the chicken stock and 2 cups of the lentils. Bring to a boil and simmer for about 10 minutes.

3. Add *A Different Color Tomato Soup*. Simmer a few minutes more to blend flavors.

4. Puree in a blender in a few batches to smooth out. Add more chicken stock if it seems dry or not "soupy" enough for you.

5. Stir in the last cup of lentils (whole) to give the soup texture.

6. Taste and add salt, to taste.

even better than jewels' lentil soup

JILL SAYS • At one of my favorite Mexican restaurants, when you order your dinner it always comes with soup. Usually it's a wonderfully tasty vegetable puree. One time dining there, I received my soup and was pleasantly surprised to see that they were serving lentil soup. As you may have figured out, we are crazy about lentils. The soup was loaded with flavor. I immediately came home and tried to re-create it.

SERVES 6–8.

  2 tablespoons extra-virgin olive oil
  1 medium onion, chopped (approximately 1 cup)
  2 cups green French lentils (*lentils de puy*)
  ¹/₂ bunch cilantro, roughly chopped (stems included)
  1 tablespoon ground cumin
  1 teaspoon salt
  8 cups organic chicken stock, vegetable stock or water

1. Place a large stockpot on the stove on medium-high heat. When the pan is warm, add the olive oil, then the onions, and sauté for 2–3 minutes, until soft and translucent.

2. Add the lentils, cilantro, cumin and salt. Continue to sauté another 2–3 minutes.

3. Add the chicken stock. Bring to a boil, skimming off any impurities. Lower heat to simmer and cook for 30–45 minutes, until the lentils are soft and the flavors meld together.

empty the crisper veggie soup

JILL SAYS • Before I started cooking for a living, I used to think making soup had to be an all-day project that required cutting and simmering for hours and hours (the way it was often made in our family). But I came to learn it's possible to make a delicious soup in no time at all—without even buying anything special! Great soup can be as easy as cleaning out the crisper and throwing the week's leftover scraps into a pot. It's a great way to keep from wasting food. Store the finished soup in the freezer and pull it out one night when you don't have time to cook.

SERVES 6–8.

1–2 tablespoons oil
2 leeks, white parts only
1 small onion
1 clove garlic, crushed
3 carrots, peeled
2 ribs celery
2 yellow zucchini or crookneck squash
1/2 red or yellow pepper

1/4 head of cauliflower
1/2 cup red lentils
1/2 teaspoon thyme leaves
6 cups vegetable stock, chicken stock or
    water
1 teaspoon salt
pinch of black pepper
dash of cayenne

1. Wash veggies and cut into large chunks.

2. Place a large stockpot on the stove over medium-high heat. When the pan is hot, add the olive oil and sauté leeks, onion and garlic until soft and transluscent, about 3–4 minutes.

3. Add the remaining vegetables and continue to sauté for another 3–4 minutes.

4. Add the lentils, thyme, salt and stock and bring to a boil. Skim off any impurities, lower heat and simmer 30–35 minutes or until veggies are soft.

5. Blend soup in batches and add black pepper and cayenne. Return to pot and reheat if necessary.

JILL'S SMART IDEA

Feel free to experiment by adding fresh or dry herbs to your soup. You can always make the soup a little heartier by throwing a handful of cooked white beans or red in with the boiling veggies. If you do, you may need to add another cup or so of stock.

all-purpose grilled-tomato soup

JEWELS SAYS • This tomato soup is light and refreshing, with a sweet, smoky flavor that features little more than just tomatoes! The trick is to grill the tomatoes over hot coals, covering them while you cook. I use a good ol' Weber BBQ with mesquite briquettes and wood chips. If you can get your hands on some Japanese tomatoes, you will find they make an amazing difference because they are super-juicy and much lower in acidity than other tomatoes. Their thin skin allows the smoky flavor to seep deep into the flesh of the tomato, giving this soup real sophistication.

Perhaps the best thing about this soup is its flexibility. I use it cold for an unusual gazpacho (a cold soup) or under fish or as a salad dressing base. Sometimes I toss it in with warm taco meat to add another layer of flavor.

the grilled-tomato puree

MAKES ABOUT 5 CUPS.

> 1 dozen Japanese tomatoes
> 3 cloves garlic, roughly chopped
> 2 shallots, roughly chopped
> 1/2 handful fresh thyme leaves
> 1/2 handful fresh savory or pinch of rosemary
> Many drizzles of extra-virgin olive oil to coat and cover tomatoes

1. Toss all ingredients in a bowl and then place tomatoes on a hot grill. Turn over as they blacken and cover grill in between turning.

2. Remove the tomatoes just before they burst. Return to the bowl with remaining bits of marinade.

3. I like to push the tomatoes and marinade through a wire food mill to strain out most of the seeds and large pieces of herbs. Doing so mashes up all the ingredients nicely and binds the flavors together.

4. If you want to skip step 3 (like Jill!), then just blend everything together.

the soup

SERVES 6–8.

　1 large onion, diced small

　$1/2$ clove garlic, diced small

　2 cups grilled-tomato puree

　$1/2$ cup chicken stock

　$1/2$ cup cooked lentils, beans, black barley, cooked chicken or shrimp (optional)

　salt, to taste

1. Sauté the onion over medium-high heat until translucent.

2. Add the garlic and sauté for ten seconds.

3. Add the tomato puree and chicken stock. Let simmer a few minutes.

4. Add salt to taste and any optional ingredients. Warm through.

JEWELS' SMART IDEA

*M*ake some extra tomato puree for the *Grilled-Tomato Vinaigrette* (page 78) and the *Grilled-Tomato Gazpacho* (page 123), or to toss in *Flap Meat Is Cheap* (page 215) or *Jewels' Favorite Soup Jill Makes* (page 131).

a different color tomato soup

JEWELS SAYS • A dinner guest once told me he did not like tomato soup—just as I was about to serve that very dish as part of an elaborate meal I had prepared for fourteen. Back to the kitchen I dashed to whip up a substitute soup for him. A short while later, the kitchen got so busy that I forgot all about it! As we were clearing the soup plates, the guest-who-hated-tomato-soup discreetly thanked me for preparing a different soup for the entire table due to his aversion. By the way, he added, "That was some of the best soup I have ever had." I had to confess my blunder and tell him he'd just enjoyed a *yellow tomato* soup. Lucky for me, he was a good sport—and very happy to have made a new discovery!

So many markets now carry beautiful yellow tomatoes. Like Japanese tomatoes, they are lower in acidity, which I prefer for some soups.

SERVES 6–8.

- 8 yellow tomatoes
- 2 shallots, peeled and quartered
- 2 cloves garlic, smashed
- 6 sprigs thyme
- several glugs extra-virgin olive oil
- 2 cups chicken stock
- salt, to taste

1. Put the tomatoes, shallots, garlic, thyme, and olive oil in a roasting pan. Roast at 400 degrees F for about 25–35 minutes or until the tomatoes are golden and juicy.

2. Remove the thyme sprigs, pulling off any thyme leaves to leave with the tomatoes.

3. Put the tomatoes and all the juice from the roasting in a food processor or through a food mill, making sure to include all the little brown bits scraped up from the bottom of the pan.

4. Blend and strain the tomato mixture through a fine-mesh strainer to remove seeds and thick skin.

5. Pour into a pan of warmed chicken stock. Simmer for 3 minutes. Add salt, to taste. Serve warm.

JEWELS' SMART IDEA

Save a cup to make *Better Than Jill's Lentil Soup* (page 114). Jill likes to use some in *Jewels' Favorite Soup Jill Makes* (page 131).

grilled-tomato gazpacho

JEWELS SAYS • For a nontraditional gazpacho, I remove the red peppers and carrots to give the smoky flavor of the *Grilled-Tomato Puree* (page 119) room to star.

It's a good idea to wear plastic kitchen gloves when cutting hot peppers; otherwise the heat from the chilis will stay on your hands, and if you touch your eyes, it will sting. Now that I have a baby, I am supersensitive about this. I don't want to touch my baby Austin's hands and risk him putting them in his mouth after cutting chilis. If you don't have gloves, plastic Baggies work in a pinch. If you make this soup for youngsters or people who are sensitive to hot foods, you can eliminate the chilis altogether.

The following ingredients can be put in a food processor on pulse setting, for a rough chop, instead of hand-dicing.

SERVES 4–6.

    2 celery stalks, diced super-small
    4 Persian cucumbers, peeled, seeded and diced super-small
    1/2 shallot, diced small
    1 green onion, chopped small
    1–2 serrano chilis, seeded and minced
    1 jalapeño chili, seeded and minced
    1/2 bunch fresh cilantro, chopped fine
    1/2 lime, juiced
    2 cups *Grilled-Tomato Puree* (page 119)
    salt and pepper, to taste

Mix all the ingredients and season to taste.

beautiful, clean albondigas soup

JEWELS SAYS • This is a little twist on Mexican meatball soup. Turkey is a great way to change it up. I prefer using dark meat turkey because I find it has more flavor.

SERVES 6–8.

THE MEATBALL MIXTURE
- a few glugs of olive oil
- $1/2$ large sweet onion, finely diced
- 1 large shallot, finely diced
- 2 handfuls shitake or crimini mushrooms, finely diced
- $1/2$ handful fresh thyme leaves
- salt and pepper, to taste
- 1 clove garlic, finely diced
- $1/2$ bunch parsley (flat-leaf or regular), finely chopped
- 2 pounds ground dark meat turkey (I also like to use $1^1/2$ pounds ground dark meat turkey and $1/2$ pound ground pork)

THE SOUP
- $1/2$ large sweet onion, diced
- 2 stalks celery, diced
- 1 large tomato, diced, or a small can of crushed tomatoes
- 8 cups chicken stock or broth
- 2 pinches Mexican oregano and/or dried cilantro
- salt, to taste

1. Prepare the meatball mixture: In a hot skillet add the oil and then sauté the onions, shallot, mushrooms, thyme, salt and pepper until mushrooms are cooked through and liquid is absorbed.

2. Add the garlic and parsley. Remove from heat and let cool.

3. Add all the sautéed ingredients to the meat, season again generously with salt and pepper and mix together lightly by hand. Be careful not to overmix, which can toughen the meat.

4. If you have time, let the meat rest for a few minutes before forming into 1" meatballs.

5. In a large-bottomed pot, brown the meatballs in olive oil, turning frequently. Set aside.

6. Prepare the soup: In the pan you used to brown the meatballs, add a touch more oil and sauté the chopped onion and celery until soft and translucent, scraping the bits from the pan to incorporate the flavors.

7. Add the fresh tomatoes and the chicken stock, oregano and cilantro to pot. Bring to a boil.

8. Turn down the heat to medium and simmer for at least 15 minutes or so.

9. Add the meatballs to the pot. Simmer until meatballs are cooked through (about 10 more minutes).

10. Add salt, to taste.

This soup gets even better the next day!

JEWELS' SMART IDEA

Save any extra uncooked meatball mixture for *Turkey Patties for Manly Men* (page 177) or *Quick Meat Sauce* (page 224).

wonton soup

JILL SAYS • To save time during the busy workweek, I always look for ways to convert leftovers into different meals. So, when I make *Chicken Potstickers* (page 237), I freeze any extra uncooked potstickers so that I can pull them out anytime to make this soup. The great thing is that you won't feel like you are eating leftovers at all.

SERVES 4–6.

- **6 cups chicken stock**
- **1 1" chunk fresh ginger, peeled**
- **16–18 uncooked *Chicken Potstickers* (page 237)**
- **2 scallions, sliced into thin diagonals**
- **2 teaspoons sesame oil**
- **1 tablespoon soy sauce**

1. Place the chicken stock and ginger in a large pot on the stove and bring to a boil. Reduce the heat and simmer for 15–20 minutes.

2. Bring the soup back up to a boil and add the wontons. Lower the heat to medium and cook for another 3–4 minutes, until wontons are cooked through.

3. Just before serving, stir in scallions, sesame oil and soy sauce.

JILL'S SMART IDEA

Cut up veggies like carrots, celery or onions and add to the soup as you are first bringing the stock and ginger to a boil. You can even throw in a handful of freshly chopped spinach when you add the scallions just before serving.

don't-knock-it cauliflower soup

JEWELS SAYS • This soup is so simple, you'd think Jill had written this recipe!

SERVES 4–6.

1 drizzle oil

1 onion, diced

1 tablespoon butter

$\frac{1}{2}$ head cauliflower, cut into tiny florets

1 box organic chicken stock

a few pinches yellow curry powder

a pinch white pepper

a pinch salt

1. In a hot pan, drizzle a little oil and begin browning the onions slightly, stirring them constantly so that they caramelize and do not burn.

2. Add the remaining ingredients and cook until the cauliflower almost falls apart.

JEWELS' SMART IDEA

Before you add the yellow curry powder, warm it in a small, dry sauté pan until it becomes aromatic. This will bring out the flavors of the curry.

jewels' favorite soup jill makes

JILL SAYS • I always keep the pantry stocked with beans, chicken stock and canned tomatoes (I prefer San Marzano). Even if I don't have time to go to the store, I can make this soup anytime. It's flavorful, hearty and healthy. When Jewels came home from the hospital after having her baby, I left this for her in her fridge. She loved it and still asks me to make it for her.

SERVES 6–8.

- 3 15-ounce cans cannelloni beans, drained and rinsed
- 6 cups chicken stock, vegetable stock or water
- 2 cloves garlic, sliced
- 2 tablespoons extra-virgin olive oil
- 1 medium onion, chopped in a medium dice
- 2 ribs celery, chopped in a medium dice
- 4 ripe tomatoes, cut into small pieces
- 1 teaspoon sea salt or kosher salt
- ¼ cup fresh parsley, roughly chopped
- 1 cup Parmesan cheese, grated

1. Place beans, stock and garlic in a large pot on the stove. Bring to boil, reduce heat to low and continue cooking for 20–30 minutes, stirring occasionally.

2. Meanwhile, heat a large skillet over medium-high heat. When the skillet is warm, add the olive oil and sauté the onion and celery for 5–6 minutes until soft and translucent. Next, add the tomatoes and salt and continue to cook another 3–4 minutes.

3. Add the vegetable mixture and parsley to beans. Cook another 15 minutes or so to meld flavors together. Serve with Parmesan cheese.

JILL'S SMART IDEAS

1. If you have any leftover *Grilled-Tomato Puree* (page 119), *Grilled-Tomato Gazpacho* (page 123) or *A Different Color Tomato Soup* (page 121), throw it into the bean soup to add more flavor.

2. If you don't have any fresh tomatoes, chop up some canned tomatoes instead.

3. Add pieces of leftover roast chicken.

4. Add some spice by throwing in ¼ teaspoon cayenne pepper when cooking the vegetables.

so-easy miso soup

JEWELS SAYS • This soup is so simple to prepare. Don't be intimidated by the seaweed, fish flakes or miso if you aren't familiar with them. Once you have made this soup, you will find it's one of the easiest delicacies to prepare! You can feel really good about it, too: The soybean protein in miso lowers cholesterol and provides you with a tremendous zap of potassium, zinc and copper!

SERVES 4–6.

2 big strips of kombu (dried seaweed for dashi)

3 cups of water

1 small handful dried Japanese fish flakes, called bonito flakes (optional)

¼ cup white miso (saikyo or shiro)

OPTIONAL ADDITIONS:

1 tablespoon soy sauce

a few small cubes of organic medium-firm tofu

a few white enoki mushrooms

1. Rinse the kombu once with water. Put kombu and water in a pot on low heat. When the water starts to boil, remove kombu and add bonito flakes (if using).

2. Immediately turn off the heat and let the flakes settle to bottom of pan. Strain the broth (called dashi) through a fine strainer, cheesecloth or kitchen muslin.

3. Stir the white miso into hot broth.

4. Add any of the optional additions, if desired—and that's it!

JEWELS' SMART IDEA

Add salmon, meat and/or veggies to the bowl for a delicious meal anytime!

"All I ever wanted to do was to make food accessible to everyone; to show that you can make mistakes—I do it all the time—but it doesn't matter."

—Jamie Oliver

deliciously different cold cucumber soup

JEWELS SAYS • Even if you don't usually like cold soups, give this one a try. My friend West treats himself to this soup every weekend during the summer. The brown mustard seeds are a trick inspired by Chef Raji Jallepalli, a genius at subtly incorporating traditional Indian spices into lots of meals. This is a great way to begin introducing the fabulous world of Indian flavors to your own family.

Variations on this soup are used throughout the book. The clean, light texture of cucumbers combines especially well with fish.

SERVES 4.

- 1 tablespoon extra-virgin olive oil
- 1 teaspoon brown mustard seeds
- 2 English cucumbers (or 6 Persian cucumbers), peeled and seeded
- 1/2 shallot, minced
- 1/4 cup buttermilk
- 3/4 cup yogurt (I prefer Greek)
- 1/4 cup crème fraîche
- 3 pinches salt

1. In a small, lidded pot or skillet, warm the oil and mustard seeds until they begin to pop. Then cover and remove from the heat.

2. Place the mustard seeds and oil in a blender and add the remaining ingredients. Pulse until blended and thick enough for soup. Serve very chilled!

JEWELS' SMART IDEA

Omit the buttermilk and add a little more crème fraîche to thicken for a yummy sauce over fish. Use any leftover soup to toss in *Cucumber Spaghetti* (page 150).

SOUP CAN CHANGE YOUR LIFE

jill's island idyll

YEARS AGO I found myself on a remote island in Fiji in a lovely *bure*—a small bungalow with a thatched roof—with few reminders of the outside world. I had traveled there to cook for a client and, during that time, met a hunky Aussie, who later became my husband. Simon was working for the sole vacation spot on the island—the idyllic Yasawa Island Resort—run by his dad. When my client went home, I stayed behind and filled in as the head chef for several of the most amazing months of my life.

Every day I oversaw the preparation of three meals for about forty guests. Meats, veggies and other ingredients were flown in on a small plane—that is, as long as arriving guests didn't bring too much luggage, in which case we might only get half of our food order or nothing at all. When we did get food, sometimes it wasn't what we'd ordered or we couldn't use it because it had been in transit for too long.

So we couldn't prepare menus ahead of time. We made do with what we had. It was excellent training for the way I make meals today from only the freshest seasonal foods, grown locally.

A fresh island market

Luckily Yasawa and the surrounding islands were a great "market." I've never tasted more delicious papaya, mango or passion fruit. The pineapple was so sweet that although I searched for that familiar acidity in its juice, I never found it. While tromping around the island, Simon would slice down a bunch of bananas and bring it back to the kitchen. We made banana bread and fruit plates like you've never tasted.

Usually my day began in the morning, when local fishermen, from the Fijian villages on the island, gathered behind the resort kitchen to try to sell me whatever they'd caught. At first they didn't know what to make of me because they were accustomed to dealing with a man. I stood on a crate in order to see everything (and keep the upper hand!) and got very good at picking out the best of the day's haul, which was usually lobster.

Cooking underground

Once a week the Fijians cooked for guests at the resort in their traditional style, similar to that of Hawaiians, using a *lovo*, which is essentially a barbecue dug into the sand. They would wrap pork, chicken or fish in banana leaves and place them on superhot rocks that had been heated in and removed from flames. Then they covered the meat with banana leaf–wrapped root vegetables like dalo and cassava, then more hot rocks, more sand and still more banana leaves. Then they would leave everything to cook slowly all day.

The meal came out so moist and with a deliciously subtle smoky flavor!

I also learned to crack coconuts and drink the fresh coconut water straight out of the shell. I copied the Fijians by sitting on a wooden board with a metallic grater screwed onto the end. Turning a half coconut in my hands around the head of the scraper, I'd grind off coconut flesh to use in many of the dishes we served.

Lest you still doubt the power of food, let me tell you about a fish called trevally that I made one night. Trevally fight so strenuously against fishing rods that people catch them more for sport than for food. Even Simon thought they were too tough to eat. But, while on Yasawa, I barbecued some trevally that came out so moist and savory, it completely won him over.

He told me later that, after taking a few bites, he thought, "This girl's *aw right!*" Eventually he followed me all the way back to my Family Kitchen in California.

go fish!

(See photos of Jill on page 137.)

JILL SAYS • On most days here in Southern California a fishmonger preps fillets for me and wraps them up in white paper. But working in Fiji gave me the chance to learn how to clean fish—big ones—with the best of them. Simon, who I met on that trip, worked on a sport fishing boat and would bring in huge catches. A couple of times I even caught the evening's dinner myself. *(See photos of Jill on page 137.)*

Sometimes the tuna or Spanish mackerel was so fresh we dispensed with cooking and simply ate it raw. It was amazing! Fiji wiped away any remaining resistance I might have harbored toward fish. Now I eat fish like an islander.

Ironically, one of the most common questions people ask us is, "How do you prepare fish?" The truth is that a fresh piece of fish requires very little preparation. In most cases you only need a hot pan and very light seasoning. Cook it for a couple of minutes on one side, flip it over and do the same on the other side. Dinner is served!

To ensure you are getting the freshest fish possible, always ask when it came in and when it was cut. Be specific about this. If you ask, "Is it fresh?" the answer will typically be yes—even if it came in a week ago. If someone in your family has had a bad experience with fish, this can be very difficult to overcome. But, if you can get them to try just one bite of really fresh, grilled fish, they'll be hooked!

go fish!

jewels' fantastic fish marinade

JEWELS SAYS • OK, I have to admit. I use this recipe a lot. I mean, a *lot*. It's a simple concoction that makes everything taste bright and fresh—not just on fish! I do use it on all kinds of fish and shrimp, first as a marinade and then I spoon some on top after it's cooked for extra flavor.

There are a few elements, I think, that make this marinade so delicious and flexible. Using zest instead of the juice prevents the fish from "cooking in the acid"—a technique used in making dishes like ceviche—so that the fish tastes like fish and not lemon. I also love fennel. It adds another layer of fresh flavor. Use a beautiful, fruity extra-virgin olive oil even though you may be tempted to get away with less. It will make all the difference between good and great.

MAKES ABOUT 1½ CUPS.

    1 shallot
    ½ bulb fennel
    1 cup extra-virgin olive oil
    zest of one lemon
    zest of one lime
    ½ teaspoon salt
    a few cranks of a pepper mill
    a few crushed pink peppercorns

OPTIONAL ADDITIONS:

    1 teaspoon curry powder (or to taste)
    a handful of fresh Italian parsley or dill
    ½ stock lemongrass, finely chopped

Cut the shallot and fennel in tiny dices (or process in a blender) and add all the other ingredients, including any optional ones you desire.

This will keep for a few days, so make a batch and use it more than once!

JEWELS' SMART IDEA

For salads, I add this marinade to red quinoa and toss it in with cucumbers or tomatoes to spice them up. It also makes a wonderful marinade to grill tomatoes.

salmon grilled on a sake-marinated cedar plank—jill's version

JILL SAYS • Cooking fish on a cedar plank gives it a subtle smoky flavor. To add even more flavor, I soak the cedar plank in sake.

SERVES 4.

1 cedar plank (available at most seafood markets and grocery stores)
1 cup water
1 cup inexpensive sake
1/2 cup hoison sauce
1 shallot, finely chopped
2 tablespoons extra-virgin olive oil
1/2 teaspoon salt
1 pound wild salmon, cut into 4 pieces
Squirts from a small bottle of water

1. Place the cedar plank in a 13" × 18" × 1" sheet tray and pour the water and sake over it. Place a heavy pan on the plank to submerge it. Allow plank to soak for at least 30 minutes.

2. In a small bowl, mix together hoison sauce, shallot, olive oil and salt. Rub half the mixture evenly over salmon pieces. Put the salmon on a plate or glass dish. Cover with plastic. Let marinate for 15–20 minutes. While the salmon is marinating, heat the barbecue.

3. Remove the cedar plank from the soaking liquid and place the salmon directly on the plank. Cook over a covered grill for about 10–15 minutes (depending on the thickness of the salmon). Occasionally open the lid to brush salmon with the remaining marinade. Be sure to keep a squirt bottle of water handy. The plank will probably catch fire around the edges before the salmon is done. Don't be alarmed; this is normal. Just squirt a little bit of water on the plank to control the flame and continue cooking.

4. Serve with forbidden rice and sautéed greens such as *Cavalo Nero* (page 279), spinach or broccoli.

JILL'S SMART IDEA

Make extra and use for *Turning Japanese–Style Breakfast* (page 59) or *Night-Before Grilled Salmon Salad for Nori* (page 197).

fancy restaurant–style salmon with maitake mushrooms— jewels' version

JEWELS SAYS • This is a simple, elegant way to serve salmon. I like to keep a little of the skin on for flavor, texture and aesthetics. Ask your fishmonger to give you a nice center cut of salmon. Cut it in half, following the line of the pinbones first. Then slice it into about 3/4" pieces. You'll need a very sharp knife to cut through the skin. This meal requires the highest-quality ingredients, but takes only moments to prepare. The trick is the timing. I've included a few hints to help time it just right.

SERVES 4–6.

1½ pounds salmon, cut into 3/4" pieces

salt and pepper, to taste

lemon zest

2 bunches asparagus

6 long chives, dipped in hot water and then in ice water to soften

a pat of butter or olive oil, for brushing on the cooked asparagus

a few glugs extra-virgin olive oil to sauté

½ shallot, sliced thin

6 clusters maitake mushroom "petals," cut from stems and separated

a few sprigs of thyme, leaves only

1. Preheat oven to 450 degrees F.

2. Season salmon pieces with salt, pepper and lemon zest. Set aside.

3. Blanch the asparagus by cooking it in boiling water until just done, then dipping it in ice water. Dry off the asparagus, divide into six bundles and tie a chive around each. Brush with butter or oil. (This can be done well ahead of time or even the night before.)

4. Heat a dry pan over medium heat. Add a glug of olive oil and sauté the shallot, mushrooms and thyme until softened.

5. Place the mushrooms in an oven-proof dish along with the asparagus bundles and cover with foil. Place the dish in the oven to keep it warm.

6. In the same pan that you sautéed the mushrooms, sear the salmon for about 2½ minutes on each side.

7. Plate the asparagus and then the mushrooms alongside the salmon.

Enjoy!

JEWELS' SMART IDEA

Make extra and use for *Turning Japanese–Style Breakfast* (page 59) or *Night-Before Grilled Salmon Salad for Nori* (page 197).

barramundi with cucumber spaghetti

JILL SAYS • The first time I tasted barramundi I thought I didn't like it because it wasn't fresh. This is a perfect example of why you must *always* buy fresh fish, because the next time I tried barramundi (when Jewels made it for me), I fell completely in love. This white fish has a firm texture, a thick skin and a mild but flavorful taste. The texture is somewhere between halibut and whitefish. What more could you ask for in a fish?

The texture of delicious beluga lentils and the cool cucumber spaghetti make this a perfectly balanced meal.

SERVES 4.

THE FISH

$^{1}/_{2}$ cup *Jewels' Fantastic Fish Marinade* (page 143) or zest of one lemon or lime

1 pound barramundi fish, cut into 4 pieces, with skin side scored

a drizzle of olive oil

salt and pepper

THE LENTILS

2 cups cooked *Lentils People Eat* (page 275)

1 shallot, very finely diced

a few glugs of extra-virgin olive oil

sea salt

8 Persian or 2 English cucumbers, peeled in stripes
a drizzle of extra-virgin olive oil
salt and pepper

1. Prepare *Jewels' Fantastic Fish Marinade*.

2. Score the skin side of the fillet in order to marinate both sides of the fish—but, more important, so that the fish does not buckle as it cooks; this can happen during cooking as the skin shrinks. You will need a sharp knife to cut through the skin, but not the fish. If your knife is not extremely sharp, ask your fishmonger to do this for you.

3. Pour the marinade over the fish to coat. Cover and refrigerate for 5 minutes to an hour.

4. Adjust a mandolin to the julienne setting (anytime you use a mandolin, be very, very careful because it is so easy to cut yourself). Julienne the cucumber and put in the fridge. (To see photo steps for using a mandolin, see *Veggie Spaghetti,* page 291).

5. Toss lentils with shallots and olive oil, and season with the sea salt. If you made them ahead of time, you can warm them in a nonstick pan for a few minutes before serving.

6. Set a dry pan over a medium-high flame until hot (about a minute). There is oil in the marinade, so you won't need extra oil in the pan. Once the pan is hot, sear the fish, skin side first, for about 4 minutes on each side. Remember to always cook the skin side first on high heat with a little olive oil so that it is nice and crispy.

7. Season the cucumber spaghetti with olive oil, salt and pepper. Spoon some lentils onto individual plates and place cooked fish over the lentils. Top the fish with cucumber.

walnut-encrusted whitefish

JILL SAYS • Jewels thought this sounded like a terrible idea. She thought the nuts would overwhelm the delicate whitefish, but she was wrong! After I made it for her she decided it was one of the best things she'd ever eaten.

You can almost make this recipe with other nuts like almonds or pecans.

SERVES 4.

- **1 cup walnuts**
- **1/2 cup flour**
- **1 egg, beaten**
- **1 1/2 teaspoon Cajun seasoning or Chef Paul Prudhomme's Blackened Redfish Magic**
- **4 6-ounce pieces of whitefish, skin on**
- **1 tablespoon extra-virgin olive oil**
- **1 tablespoon butter**
- **1/2 lemon**

1. Preheat the oven to 400 degrees F.

2. Place the walnuts in a food processor and pulse until finely chopped. You can also finely chop by hand if you do not own a food processor.

3. Place the walnuts, flour and egg in three separate shallow dishes (pie plates work well).

4. Season the flour with 1/2 teaspoon Cajun seasoning.

5. Season fish evenly on both sides with remaining Cajun seasoning.

6. Dip flesh side of fish first in flour, shaking off any excess. Then dip in egg and, finally, in walnuts. Set aside on a plate. Repeat with the rest of the fish.

7. Heat an oven-safe skillet large enough to accommodate all the fish over medium-high heat and add the oil and butter. Sauté the fish, walnut side down, for 2–3 minutes, watching carefully so as not to burn the nuts. When the nuts are nicely browned, flip the fish over and continue cooking for another 3–4 minutes or until skin is crispy.

8. Transfer the pan of fish to the oven to finish cooking. Squeeze a bit of lemon juice over the fish and serve immediately.

grilled halibut with red quinoa

JEWELS SAYS • I believe halibut is one of the easiest fish to like. I use it as my "starter" fish for nonfish eaters and kids. It is so important to make the fish experience a good one for someone new to fish!

Halibut works for grilling, which provides fantastic results. But, although I love my grill, I have to admit it is even easier to cook in a pan. I use the restaurant technique of searing both sides in a pan and then finishing the fish in the oven. With a great pan, you can sear the fish and put the entire pan in the oven as you plate up the remainder of the meal. *When you take the pan out of the oven, it is very, very important that you remember to use a thick towel or mitt because the handle will be just as hot as the pan and you can seriously burn yourself.* After the pan is out of the oven, it is still easy to forget and grab that superheated handle, so I keep the towel or mitt on it until it has cooled!

I serve this quinoa to add great texture. The sweet flavor of the yams works really well with the fish!

SERVES 4–6.

THE FISH

> 1/2 cup *Jewels' Fantastic Fish Marinade* (page 143)
>
> 1 1/2 pounds halibut

THE QUINOA

> 2 cups plain cooked quinoa (from *Quinoa with Crunchy Veggies and Fresh Herbs* [page 293])
>
> 1/4 cup *Jewels' Fantastic Fish Marinade*

THE YAMS

> 2 whole yams, cut into 1/4" disks
>
> 6 thyme sprigs, leaves only, chopped fine
>
> 1/2 rosemary sprig, leaves only, chopped fine
>
> salt and pepper
>
> 1/2 cup extra-virgin olive oil
>
> 1/4 cup fresh squeezed orange juice (optional)

1. If using a grill, light it so it has a chance to get nice and hot.

2. Prepare *Jewels' Fantastic Fish Marinade* and pour 1/2 cup of marinade over halibut. Cover the fish and let it marinate in the refrigerator for 5 minutes to 1 hour.

3. In a medium-sized mixing bowl, toss the yam disks in with herbs, salt and pepper, oil and orange juice. Grill until soft on the barbecue or in a grill pan on the stove. Place on a plate and cover with foil to keep warm.

4. Toss the quinoa with ¼ cup fish marinade (you can serve this warm or cold, but I prefer room temperature).

5. Remove the fish from the marinade and grill until opaque. Serve with the quinoa and yams.

JEWELS' SMART IDEA

Make extra quinoa for *Quinoa with Crunchy Veggies and Fresh Herbs* (page 293). With leftover fish and quinoa, you can use some avocado to make yummy *Nori Wraps (Japanese Burritos)* (page 197).

jewels' cabo san lucas ceviche

JEWELS SAYS • This recipe makes me think of sitting in a small Mexican restaurant, sandy from the beach, with salt still in my hair—and around the rim of my margarita glass. *Mmmm.* Heaven!

Because this fish is cooked only by the acid in the lime juice, it is very important that the fish be the freshest it can possibly be.

SERVES 4–6.

THE FISH

¹/₂ pound cold-water shrimp, cut small (try not to use tiger shrimp,
  as they tend to be mushy for ceviche)

¹/₂ pound fresh day-boat scallops, cleaned of the feet and cut small

¹/₂ pound halibut or sea bass, cut small

THE CEVICHE MARINADE

6 limes, juiced

2 blood oranges, juiced (optional)

1 serrano chili, sliced thin

1 jalapeño chili, cut thin

a big pinch of kosher salt

THE CEVICHE JUICE

1 cup *Salsa* (page 62)

a few shakes of your favorite hot sauce (like Tapatío)

or

1 cup *Grilled-Tomato Puree* (page 119), chilled

1 shot Patrón Silver tequila, chilled

THE CEVICHE SALAD

2 avocados, diced

1 stalk celery, diced

¹/₂ bunch cilantro, chopped

a few big glugs extra-virgin olive oil

1. Prepare the ceviche marinade: Mix all the ingredients in a bowl large enough to accommodate the fish.

2. Place the fish pieces in the bowl with the ceviche marinade and let sit in the refrigerator for about 30 minutes, stirring every 10 minutes to cook the fish evenly in the juice. The fish is cooked when it has changed from translucent to white and opaque.

3. While the fish is marinating, prepare the ceviche juice of your choice.

4. Prepare the ceviche salad: Toss all the ingredients together.

5. Drain the marinade off the fish and add the ceviche juice. Then toss gently with the ceviche salad. Serve right away with tortilla chips and a good margarita!

JEWELS' SMART IDEA

To make a nontraditional ceviche, use leftover shrimp or fish and salsa or *Grilled-Tomato Puree* (page 119).

"Good food depends almost entirely on good ingredients."

—Alice Waters

how to feed a hungry man

(who wants to keep his six-pack)

JILL SAYS • My husband, Simon, earned a unique nickname after one of our neighbors watched him cleaning out our yard to make room for a vegetable garden.

"I kept thinking, What's he going to do about that tree stump?" our neighbor told me later. "The next thing I knew, Bam Bam pulled it up, threw it over his shoulder and carried it away!"

Bam Bam, indeed! Simon works so hard that he can eat anything—anything—and his pants still fall off his waist. Sure, I get jealous, but the truth is I love it. I love food so much that it's wonderful having a husband who will always, always consume more than me!

Satisfying a hungry man and keeping him healthy at the same time can be a challenge. Luckily, Bam Bam likes to eat good stuff. We both understand that the key to healthy living is balance. For us, this means we do have pasta once in a while. But, if we make steak for dinner, then we eat it with fresh tomatoes and pan-roasted cauliflower cooked in olive oil, instead of mashed potatoes made with cream and butter.

The more colorful your meal is, chances are, the better it is for you. So, try to include greens like *cavalo nero* (black kale or Tuscan kale) or spinach and use mashed yams or roasted butternut squash as a super-tasty alternative to potatoes. This doesn't mean never eating mashed potatoes, just not frequently. Have a delicious turkey burger instead of eating red meat. Skip the bread and wrap it in lettuce. What I love about the meals in this chapter is that I can feel good about giving them to my hungry man—and I can still eat them myself.

When I make the shrimp pasta for dinner, I sometimes skip the pasta myself and just eat the shrimp, tomatoes and arugula—still a completely satisfying meal. After all, if my hungry man is going to have a six-pack, I want to look good, too! More important, I want us both to feel great and stay healthy.

JEWELS SAYS • The one time I couldn't stop myself from cooking is when I started dating Akihiko Frank Washington, also known as Kiko. Maybe it was because he turned out to be a Barry Manilow fan like me (and can sing his "Very Strange Medley" straight through, which is just incredibly impressive!). Or maybe it was because he's traveled the world and loves foods from all cultures, as I do. Or maybe it was any one of a million other things—but I just could *not* stop making this man food.

When Kiko came home from business trips, I knew he'd be wanting something healthy and home-cooked, so I'd leave on his front doorstep boxes containing dishes like (the one I now call) *Kiko's Succulent Pork Chops* (page 173), *Turkey Patties for Manly Men* (page 177) and *A Man's Short Rib Stew* (page 167).

West, the "other man" in my life, who works with me and is like a brother, thought I was seriously overdoing it. "You *cannot* give that to him," West would insist. "You are going to scare him away!"

But I couldn't stop. I just had to get all this cooking for Kiko out of my system. "Here!" I'd say, throwing up my hands and sending West home with everything I'd made for Kiko that day (for the record, West did not complain about this second part).

It turns out that West, however, was half right. Each time Kiko returned from a trip, the meals he found on his stoop made him *very* uncomfortable. He harbored a very Japanese resistance to receiving gifts, but unable to resist, he'd devour the contents! Pretty soon, and despite the fact that he still felt guilty, he started wondering what might be sitting on his porch even before he'd grabbed his luggage off the baggage carousel.

The *real* reason for Kiko's initial resistance, I think, is that he could feel the forty-eight-year-old walls of his bachelorhood beginning to crumble. Eventually I wore him down. And now I cook for both of us—and our son, Austin—at home in our own Family Kitchen.

how to feed
a hungry man
(who wants to keep his six-pack)

the occasional pasta

JEWELS AND JILL SAY • Jill's favorite thing about this dish is the light and delicate egg noodle pasta. The brand we love is called Spinosi (see Resources, page 307). We do not believe anyone should deprive themselves by cutting out major food groups. Instead we believe in balance in the way we live and what and how we eat—so there's nothing wrong with enjoying the occasional pasta!

SERVES 4–6.

- 8 ounces tagliolini or spaghettini
- 2 tablespoons extra-virgin olive oil
- 1 medium clove garlic, finely minced
- 1 pound medium-sized raw shrimp, peeled and deveined
- 8 Roma tomatoes, peeled, seeded and chopped (or just seeded and chopped)
- 1 teaspoon lemon zest
- salt and pepper
- 2 large handfuls baby arugula
- 2 teaspoons parsley, roughly chopped
- 1/4 cup almonds, toasted and chopped
- 1/4 cup Parmesan cheese

1. Bring a large pot of salted water to boil and cook pasta.

2. Meanwhile, heat a large skillet over medium-high heat. Add olive oil and sauté garlic for one minute, being careful not to burn it. Add shrimp and sauté for another minute or two. Add tomatoes and lemon zest and continue cooking until tomatoes are warm and shrimp has cooked through. Remove pan from heat and set aside.

3. By this time the pasta should be cooked. Drain pasta and mix together with warm shrimp-and-tomato mixture. Season with salt and pepper and mix in the fresh arugula, parsley and nuts. Serve with Parmesan cheese.

JEWELS AND JILL'S SMART IDEA

Skinny Minnies can eat this dish without the pasta—it's still a delicious and satisfying meal!

a man's short-rib stew

JEWELS SAYS • I often receive calls from my cousin Mandy just before the dinner hour, asking me for ideas for what she should make for dinner. Her husband, Brian, is a firefighter whose job sometimes keeps him away from home for weeks at a time. When he returns, he is exhausted and hungry and needs to feel the comfort of home. On one of his homecomings, I gave her this recipe and it has become his traditional welcome-home meal. Now Brian even makes it for the guys at the firehouse!

SERVES 4–6.

oil, to brown meat

8 beef short ribs, seasoned with salt, pepper and a bit of garlic powder

1 large onion, diced medium

1 clove garlic, crushed

2 shallots, sliced

1 large can crushed tomatoes and juice (or 3 fresh)

6 cups beef stock

1/2 cup black barley (or 1 potato or a handful of rice)

salt, to taste

2 carrots, peeled and diced

3 stalks celery, cut in chunks

1/4 head cabbage, cut in chunks

1. Heat a large-bottom stockpot on medium-high heat. Add a few glugs of oil and brown the ribs on all sides. You may have to do them in batches. Set ribs aside.

2. In same pot, sauté the onion, garlic and shallots for about a minute or two, scraping the bottom bits to incorporate their flavors. Return the ribs to pan.

3. Stir for a moment; then add tomatoes, stock and barley. Season with salt, to taste. Bring to a boil and skim off any impurities.

4. Reduce heat and let simmer, partially covered, for about an hour and a half. If you need more liquid, you can add more water or a little more beef stock.

5. Add the carrots and celery. If you are using rice or potato, put it in now. Continue to cook for another 30 minutes. Then add the cabbage and cook another 15–20 minutes. By now the meat will be tender and the barley soft.

This stew, like most, is even better the next day!

"Noncooks think it's silly to invest two hours' work in two minutes' enjoyment; but if cooking is evanescent, so is the ballet."

—Julia Child

bam bam's favorite steak dinner

JILL SAYS • Bam Bam really is the perfect name for my husband, Simon. He is strong and rough and has a huge appetite. Some nights, he comes home from work terrifically hungry and we make dinner in a hurry to feed him fast! I have always loved the taste of steak with fresh tomatoes, so instead of taking the time to make a salad, I just slice up some juicy tomatoes. By the time he has finished grilling the steaks, I have the plates ready with pan-roasted cauliflower and beautiful tomatoes with Gorgonzola.

SERVES 4–6.

4 T-bone steaks

1–2 tablespoons extra-virgin olive oil

salt, pepper and garlic powder

2 large ripe tomatoes, thickly sliced

4 tablespoons soft Gorgonzola cheese

1 tablespoon parsley, roughly chopped

1 tablespoon extra-virgin olive oil

Pan-Roasted Cauliflower (page 280)

1. Heat either the grill, a grill pan, the broiler or a cast-iron skillet. Rub the steaks with olive oil. Season generously with salt, pepper and garlic powder. Let sit for 5 minutes or so. Cook steaks to desired doneness. When cooked, let steaks rest for another 5 minutes or so before serving.

2. Divide sliced tomatoes evenly among 4 plates. Sprinkle Gorgonzola and parsley evenly over tomatoes. Season with salt and pepper and drizzle olive oil over tomatoes.

3. Plate the steaks and serve with *Pan-Roasted Cauliflower*.

JILL'S SMART IDEA

Split the cooking up! Most guys love to grill, so cut your prep time in half by letting them do it—and make it fun for everyone. Save leftover steak for *Smart Idea Burritos* (page 187) or *Don't Waste Food—Make Fried Rice!* (page 57).

kiko's succulent pork chops

JEWELS SAYS • My husband, Kiko, says that back when we were dating, these pork chops, in particular, got him thinking about what it would be like to share a Family Kitchen together one day. Yes, I did win my man's heart through his stomach! Now that we have cooked together for a few years, these pork chops have become one of his trusted standbys. I hate to admit it, but I think he makes them better than I do!

The secret ingredient here is the Japanese or kurobuta pork. It is so moist and tender that, once you eat it, it will spoil you for any other kind of pork. If you do not find these chops, ask your butcher. He may be able to order them for you. I have also ordered them online (see Resources, page 303). If you cannot get them, then use any other thick, good-quality chop.

SERVES 4.

    4 kurobuta pork chops, seasoned with salt, pepper and a bit of garlic powder.

    If you have time you can also season with:

        6 sprigs of thyme, leaves only

        5–6 sage leaves, torn

        a handful of parsley, chopped

        $1/2$ shallot, chopped (use the other half to sauté mushrooms)

        zest of $1/2$ lemon (I use a microplane)

        $1/2$ shallot chopped

    extra-virgin olive oil to sauté

    a few handfuls of shitake mushrooms, stems removed and torn into pieces

    salt and pepper

    $1/2$ small butternut squash, cut into small chunks

    a splash of good cognac, applejack, Maker's Mark whiskey or calvados (optional)

1. Preheat oven to 375 degrees F.

2. Heat an oven-proof pan over medium-high heat. Once the pan is hot, brown the seasoned pork chops on both sides. Remove and set aside.

3. Pour a glug of oil in the pan to cook the mushrooms, seasoning with salt and pepper.

4. Add the squash and mix with the mushrooms. Add about $1/2$ cup of water and cook until evaporated, scraping the bits from the bottom of the pan.

5. Return the chops to pan.

6. If using the liquor, pour in the pan and flambé. Cook until the flame fully disappears.

7. Transfer the pan to oven for about 15–20 minutes, or until the chops are just barely pink inside and the squash is soft.

JEWELS' SMART IDEA

Save leftover pork chop for *Smart Idea Burritos* (page 187) or *Don't Waste Food—Make Fried Rice!* (page 57).

"I wouldn't keep him around long if I didn't feed him well."

—Julia Child

turkey patties for manly men

JEWELS SAYS • It seems that whenever I order a turkey burger in a restaurant, I'm disappointed. They are often heavy and lack flavor. The key ingredient to this version is that I add tiny bits of chopped mushrooms and parsley into the ground turkey, which adds moisture and flavor. The taste of the mushroom is so subtle that even kids will love them! These burgers are so satisfying that my husband makes them and uses lettuce instead of buns. This is one way we eat a little less white flour.

SERVES 4–6.

1 recipe of *Meatball Mixture* (page 125), formed into patties instead of meatballs

1 head of red-leaf lettuce, leaves separated to use as "buns"

a few slices of tomato

a few slices of pickle

ketchup

mustard

a few slices of avocado

whatever else you like on your burger! I like using the *Pickled Red Onion* (page 85) for a little kick!

Heat a nonstick pan or light the grill. If cooking on the stove, add a glug of oil once the pan is hot and cook through, flipping once halfway through. Serve with the rest of the ingredients.

JILL'S SMART IDEA

This same *Meatball Mixture* is used in the *Beautiful, Clean Albondigas Soup* (page 125) and in the *Quick Meat Sauce* (page 224). So when you make one mixture, you can use it at least three different ways! Break up the cooked turkey patty and put it on top of a salad.

papa's chicken

JILL SAYS • I love crispy pan-roasted chicken. Although marinating chicken is a great way to add flavor, herbs in the marinade burn during the pan-roasting process, producing a bitter taste. I found a solution to this problem by browning the chicken first, then rubbing it with the herb mixture and putting it in the oven to finish cooking. The result is crispy and juicy roasted chicken that is full of flavor. It tastes like you have marinated it overnight.

SERVES 4–6.

8 chicken leg and thigh pieces
salt and pepper

HERB MIXTURE:

2 tablespoons fresh flat-leaf parsley, finely chopped

2 teaspoons fresh rosemary, finely chopped

1 teaspoon fresh thyme leaves, finely chopped

1 tablespoon garlic, finely chopped

2–3 tablespoons extra-virgin olive oil

1 tablespoon extra-virgin olive oil

1/2 lemon

1. Season the chicken with salt and pepper and set aside. Meanwhile, make the herb mixture by stirring all ingredients together in a small bowl.

2. Preheat oven to 400 degrees F.

3. Heat a large skillet over medium-high heat. When the pan is hot, add the olive oil. Place the chicken in the pan—you may have to work in batches—skin side down. When the chicken is nicely browned, after 4–5 minutes, turn over and brown the other side. You will know when the chicken is ready to be turned when it can be easily removed from the pan. If it sticks to the pan, it's not ready to be turned. Continue browning on the other side. Remove the chicken from the pan and place it on a large sheet tray.

4. When the chicken has cooled slightly—just long enough so you won't burn yourself, usually about 2 minutes—rub the herb mixture all over chicken on both sides.

5. Place the chicken in the oven, skin side up, and cook for another 30 minutes or so. Remove from the oven and immediately squeeze the lemon over the chicken pieces.

JILL'S SMART IDEA

Use extra chicken to make *Don't Waste Food—Make Fried Rice!* (page 57) or *Smart Idea Burritos* (page 187). Add to any soup.

i gotta run!

JILL SAYS • When we were kids, if we had to leave the house early in the morning, Nana would not let us out the door without breakfast. She pressed small, beautifully prepared burritos, wrapped in foil, into our hands. Often they contained tasty leftovers from the fridge that were still cold or that she had warmed up for us.

In our way-too-busy lifestyle, you can just imagine how often we hear the phrase "I gotta run!" Like Nana, we don't let family members leave our kitchens without something to eat on the go. Ideally, we would eat every meal sitting down. But, since that's just not gonna happen, we do as Nana did.

Since we grew up in a house where you could always find a tortilla, we keep some around. Whole-wheat tortillas are wonderful, but we also wrap food in nori (seaweed paper), rice paper and lettuce. You'd be surprised to discover what tastes delicious in a wrap: chicken salad, beef brisket, fish, vegetable sautés. The list is endless. Sometimes we add some cooked beans for protein or a dash of shredded cheese.

While we think it's really important to eat meals sitting down, we know it's not always possible. But running out the door doesn't have to mean skipping a meal. You will be surprised at how much energy and focus you have when you actually give your body what it needs throughout the day—even when you just gotta run.

i gotta run!

nana's egg-and-potato burritos

JILL SAYS • When we were kids, whether we were going on a school field trip or a long car ride, our nana never let us leave the house without taking something with us. She would get up extra early to make homemade tortillas. She wrapped each burrito in foil, marking the ones with green chili by twisting the tin foil in a special way. This is a tradition our family carries on today. If we are going on a road trip or an early-morning car ride, someone (usually Mom) hands us a brown paper bag filled with these delicious egg-and-potato burritos.

SERVES 4–6.

 1 tablespoon olive oil
 1 large russet or 2 medium white rose potatoes, peeled and julienned
 salt and pepper
 $\frac{1}{2}$ medium onion, sliced thin
 8 large eggs, beaten
 2 jalapeño chilis, roasted, peeled and chopped (optional)
 6 medium-sized flour tortillas, slightly warmed

1. Heat the oil in a large nonstick skillet over medium-high heat. Add the potatoes, season with salt and pepper and sauté until soft and barely brown. Don't overstir or they will turn mushy.

2. Add onions and sauté 2–3 minutes more, until the onions are soft.

3. Add the beaten eggs and jalapeños (if using). Cook until the eggs are just done.

4. Divide mixture evenly among the tortillas. Roll them up, wrap them in foil and enjoy!

smart idea burritos

JILL SAYS • Whenever we had any kind of meat leftover, our nana would turn it into delicious burritos, using the juice from the tomatoes to keep the meat moist. They were so tasty, served plain without cheese, sour cream or guacamole. You can feel free to add any extras that sound good to you. My favorite way to eat them is plain with a dash of hot sauce, like Nana used to make them.

SERVES 4–6.

- 1–2 tablespoons extra-virgin olive oil
- 1 medium onion, sliced
- 2–3 heaping cups leftover meat, such as steak, roast beef, pork or chicken, cut into chunks or thin slices
- 2 medium ripe tomatoes, cut into medium-sized chunks
- ¼ cup cilantro, roughly chopped
- salt and pepper
- 4–6 medium-sized flour tortillas

OPTIONAL ADDITIONS:

- *Salsa* (page 62) and *Guacamole* (page 63)
- sour cream
- cheese
- hot sauce

1. Heat a large skillet over medium-high heat. When the pan is hot, add the olive oil and sauté the onions for 2 minutes or so, until soft.

2. Add the meat, tomatoes and cilantro. Season with salt and pepper and sauté for another 3–4 minutes, until the tomatoes are soft and the meat is warm.

3. Divide the mixture evenly among the tortillas, roll them in foil and take them with you!

mushroom quesadillas
on whole-wheat tortillas

JEWELS SAYS • You can feel pretty good about eating these delicious quesadillas. I make them on whole-wheat tortillas or Indian *chapati* and I use only cheese that I grate or crumble myself. It is so much more costly to buy pregrated cheese. Unfortunately, in order to keep the cheese from sticking together in the package, potato starch or other anticaking powders are added. By using unprocessed cheese, you give yourself and your family a chance to digest your food much more quickly. I try to use a little bit of cheese and lots of greens and mushrooms.

SERVES 4–6.

> **kosher salt**
>
> **4 whole-wheat tortillas**
>
> **a few handfuls of assorted, grated cheeses: options include *cotija*, feta, goat or farmer's cheese**
>
> **a few handfuls of spinach, or cooked *Cavalo Nero* (page 279)**
>
> **assorted mushrooms, sautéed in a bit of olive oil, salt, pepper and fresh thyme**

1. Heat a pan on medium-high heat. Sprinkle a little kosher salt (in this case it must be coarse salt) in the pan and put one tortilla on top. This will keep it from sticking to the pan and help to crisp it up, without using any oil.

2. Place the cheese and fillings on half of the tortilla.

3. Fold the tortilla in half, cooking one side first and then the other. Repeat with remaining tortillas.

JILL'S SMART IDEA

This is a great snack to leave in the fridge and reheat later in a pan. I prefer not to use the microwave because it melts the cheese too much and makes the tortilla chewy.

smart idea sandwich spreads (four kinds!)

JEWELS AND JILL SAY • Since the no-carb craze, sandwiches get a bad rap. We have a few tips for eating guilt-free sandwiches: Use whole-grain breads, pita or tortillas. Instead of lettuce, try to use a darker green, such as baby spinach, arugula, beet greens or pea greens. Instead of mayo, try a healthier spread.

tomato chutney spread

MAKES 4–5 CUPS.

- 1 tablespoon extra-virgin olive oil
- 1 large onion, diced
- 6 large ripe tomatoes, chopped into small pieces
- 2 Fuji apples, grated
- $\frac{1}{2}$ teaspoon garlic, minced
- $\frac{1}{2}$ teaspoon ginger, minced
- $\frac{3}{4}$ cup red or white wine vinegar
- 1 tablespoon salt
- $\frac{3}{4}$ cup brown sugar
- $\frac{1}{4}$ teaspoon cinnamon
- $\frac{1}{2}$ teaspoon dry mustard
- $\frac{1}{4}$ teaspoon cayenne pepper
- 1 teaspoon curry powder
- 1 cup golden or dark raisins

1. Heat a medium-sized pan on the stove over medium-high heat. When the pan is warm, add the olive oil and sauté the onion until soft and translucent, approximately 2–3 minutes.

2. Add the remaining ingredients. Bring to a boil, reduce heat and simmer until the chutney is thick, stirring occasionally. I like to cook this for a few hours, but you can get away with doing it for a shorter time if you wish.

3. Store in airtight jars in the fridge, or seal in hot sterile jars to keep even longer.

This will keep for two weeks.

olive spread

MAKES 1¼ CUPS.

1 cup olives, pits removed (use your favorite kind or a mixture of your favorites)
2 tablespoons extra-virgin olive oil
1 small shallot, very finely diced
1 tablespoon parsley, roughly chopped

Put all the ingredients in the bowl of a food processor and pulse until finely chopped. If you do not own a food processor, use a sharp knife to finely chop everything.

This will keep for one week.

roasted poblano chili spread

MAKES 1 CUP.

4 fresh poblano chilis
a small handful of cilantro
1 shallot, very finely diced
¼ teaspoon minced garlic (optional)
2 tablespoons extra-virgin olive oil
salt, to taste

1. Roast the chilis. Remove and discard the peel and seeds. (See *Do-It-Ahead Chicken Chiles Rellenos* [page 262–263] for photo steps.)

2. Put the chilis and the remaining ingredients in bowl of a food processor and pulse until finely chopped. If you do not own a food processor, use a sharp knife to finely chop everything.

This will keep for one week.

avocado-mustard spread

MAKES ½ CUP.

1 Haas avocado (or any kind of avocado)
2 tablespoons Dijon mustard
a pinch of nutmeg
a pinch of coriander
salt and pepper

1. Peel, remove the pit and mash the avocado.

2. Stir in the remaining ingredients.

This should be eaten the day you make it.

fish sandwich with pea tendrils wrapped in parchment

JEWELS SAYS • Finding new ways for your family to use the contents of your fridge will save you time and money. The more you cook with your family, the more comfortable and creative they will become using leftovers to create a delicious meal. This sandwich is one way to use a piece of fish from the night before, with some leftover *Deliciously Different Cold Cucumber Soup* (page 135) and some of the *Pickled Red Onion* (page 85) used in the salad. Pea tendrils are becoming more available in mainstream markets and are a fresh way to add something new and healthy to your list of greens! You can wrap it all up in parchment paper. Eating on the run was never so tasty or good for you!

SERVES 2.

- 1 piece of cooked fish
- 2 slices of bread, lightly toasted or grilled (you can substitute lettuce)
- a handful of pea tendrils, sautéed in a bit of olive oil, salt and pepper
- a few tablespoons *Deliciously Different Cold Cucumber Soup* (page 135) with a dollop of crème fraîche added to thicken
- a few *Pickled Red Onions* (page 85)
- sea salt, to season (I like to use olive salt! Yum!)

Make a sandwich and wrap it in parchment to go!

JEWELS' SMART IDEA

If you don't want to use bread, make a fish burrito by wrapping it in a whole-wheat tortilla or nori.

nori wraps
(japanese burritos)

JILL SAYS • Nori is loaded with important minerals and is also full of fiber. You can eat salad on the run just by wrapping it in nori. I love to make a salad out of leftover salmon to put in nori, but you can use anything. Tuna salad is also a great choice. Jewels cuts up raw veggies and wraps them in nori with a little quinoa and avocado for a healthy snack on the go.

night-before grilled salmon salad for nori

SERVES 2–4.

  8 ounces leftover grilled salmon

  2 tablespoons red onion, finely chopped

  1 tablespoon cilantro, finely chopped

  1 tablespoon mayonnaise (or just enough to hold salad together)

  a squeeze of lemon juice

  salt and pepper

  4 sheets nori

  a handful of greens, such as baby lettuce or pea sprouts

1. Use a fork to flake the salmon and mix it together with the remaining ingredients.

2. Divide the salad and greens evenly among the nori sheets. Roll them up tightly and off you go!

JEWELS' SMART IDEA

I like to use leftover *Deliciously Different Cold Cucumber Soup* (page 135) instead of mayo.

nuts to keep you from going nuts

JILL SAYS • I used to have a really bad habit of letting myself get too hungry in between meals. I could feel my blood sugar dropping and watch myself become impatient, tired and struggling to concentrate. I've found that just by snacking on some nuts, which are a great source of protein, I can avoid the LBS (low-blood-sugar) blues to stay focused and energetic.

MAKES 2 CUPS.

> 1 tablespoon olive oil
>
> 2 cups raw nuts (Use a mixture of your favorites. I go heavy on almonds, which are high in protein.)
>
> 3 tablespoons furikake (an Asian mixture of sesame seeds, chopped noris and other ingredients—you can usually purchase this in the Asian section of your grocery store)

1. Preheat oven to 350 degrees F.

2. Mix the olive oil with the nuts to coat them evenly. Spread the nuts on a sheet tray and bake until nicely browned, approximately 10–12 minutes.

3. Remove the nuts from oven and allow to cool slightly. Mix the nuts together with furikake and store in an airtight container.

JILL'S SMART IDEA

Instead of using the furikake, sometimes I just roast the nuts and, right before eating, add a handful of dried fruit. It's better to add the fruit at the last minute because the moisture from the fruit can make the nuts chewy.

jewels and baby

IT'S STRANGE to say, but the day I knew I would become a mother myself was the day Jill called, in tears of joy, to say *she* was pregnant. After looking forward to becoming a mother for so long, it was finally happening for her and Simon. At the time, Kiko and I were undergoing fertility treatments, which required that I give myself shots every morning. It was pretty intense. But as Jill shared her good news, I felt my own worries drain away. It's difficult to explain why, but we've always done everything together, so it made sense that we would do motherhood together, too. "Wow," I remember us saying to each other. "Here we go." Six months later, I was pregnant, too.

When I couldn't cook

I spent the last two months of my pregnancy on bed rest—a pretty unnatural state for this Family Chef! In my whole life I had never sat still before. Kiko would come home after a full day at work and

I'd say, "Today, I'm making a brain." Or "I'm putting together organs in a little person's body." I don't think I've ever moved so little to accomplish so much! Becoming a mother was a big thing for me. And, because I'm a Family Chef, it turned my world upside down.

Right after giving birth, I could no more make my new family dinner than make myself a cup of coffee. And the man I'd won over with food? Instead of us cooking together, he was forced to assume the place of the Family Chef on his own. People would say to Kiko, "I can't believe you'll cook for Jewels. That must be so intimidating!" But he was really motivated to step into the role and help, even at the end of a long workday. All he wanted was a little direction, so I dragged a chair into the kitchen to coach him through dinner as I nursed Austin. It was nice being there in the Family Kitchen, keeping him company, during the only time of the day we got to spend together. It wasn't just a job for him, since we both care passionately about the food we put into our bodies (and saving money by eating in all the time gave him an added thrill).

To really get him comfortable, we got smart and put a television in the kitchen. He finds it relaxing to watch sports while washing the dishes. I say whatever it takes to make your Family Kitchen welcoming is worth doing! Pretty soon, Kiko was cooking like a pro and now we take turns. As Austin got a little bigger, we would set him on the kitchen counter in a little bouncy chair. He looks so cute in it! He gets to watch us up close as we cook, seeing and smelling everything we do. I love that.

Growing into motherhood

As women, we are so strong and so capable of doing so many wonderful things. I believe that every experience we have can make us that much stronger and more beautiful.

Growing into motherhood is a journey for me. I feel very fortunate to have the strength every day to serve my family, be a great partner to Kiko and be committed to my career. And I'm enjoying all the surprises along the way. Before Austin, I used to think nothing could be as rewarding as spending eight days preparing an elaborate dinner party. But I was wrong. After blending together a simple mixture of smashed yams and quinoa, I'm just as high because my eater, my very own little boy, is totally happy and satisfied. What could be better?

a lotta mouths to feed

JEWELS SAYS • When we were kids, ten or even twenty people would often turn up, unexpectedly, for dinner. In our family, it was never a problem. Stretching meals creatively is something Nana, our mother and the two of us would do often. Our pantry shelves and freezers always contain a couple key extra foods that we can use when we need to be creative.

It's a skill that comes in handy as a Family Chef.

One year I traveled with my client to France for the Cannes Film Festival and we stayed at the Hotel du Cap. The hotel staff wasn't thrilled to have me underfoot in their kitchen, preparing meals, so they sent me to a basement kitchen that, I swear, had to have been two hundred years old. After a day of cooking, I was cleaning up. I had just a few things left, including some baguettes, a couple of cheeses and two steak fillets, when I got a message from my client requesting that I prepare something for him to eat. "He's really hungry," I was told. "Kind of make it a lot."

Hmmm, I thought. I began slicing the meat very, very thinly. The plate I sent up went over so well that, another message came down: Could I make more? No matter what I sent up, I got yet another request for still more: "Your food is making him so *happy*! He is loving it! Could you make more?"

Nothing motivates me more than delighting the people I feed and so, somehow, I did. I hardly remember what I prepared. I do recall slicing bread extra-thin and using prosciutto to build sandwiches that stacked tall on the plate so they looked bigger than they were. After cooking the few prawns I had, and arranging them on a plate with greens for a salad, I threw the shells in a pot with some vegetable scraps to make a soup.

After a couple of hours of this, I got a last message: "He'd like to see you. Could you come up?"

Really? I thought. For once I was wearing my chef whites. (This was France, after all.) Grubby and dirty, I walked across the gleaming hotel lobby as guests in formal wear crossed my path.

As the door to his hotel room opened, I was astonished to see my client and what looked like about twenty of his friends giving me a round of applause. He knew I wasn't exactly prepared to serve an impromptu dinner for a group of that size, but he also knew me well enough to know just what buttons to push to get me to pull it off (without scaring me in the process!).

After growing up in Rocky's kitchen, I just know instinctively how to stretch a meal for all it's worth.

At home, the best way we've found for doing so is keeping it simple. Make a one-pot wonder like *Jewels' Delicioso Arróz Con Pollo* (page 209). Or heat up a bowl of chopped green chilis, sautéed with onions and tomato—a mixture our family puts in everything and keeps lots of in the freezer. Take a soup and turn it into a meal.

The recipes in this chapter can be easily prepared and stretched to feed plenty of people without taking forever, or breaking the bank.

a lotta mouths to feed

everyone loves chili

JEWELS SAYS • When people ask for something easy they can make for a big gathering, I always suggest chili. If you make it from scratch and use good-quality meat, it is a decadent meal. Once a year a friend of mine throws a big party and we make all different kinds of chili, serving them up out of big cast-iron pots with all the fixin's. Eating together this way sets a casual and relaxed tone as everyone serves themselves and chats with fellow eaters! The same thing happens when you make chili with friends. Chopping ingredients and tasting chili along the way just tends to be a bonding experience.

SERVES 10–12.

THE MEAT

> extra-virgin olive oil
> 3 pounds beef sirloin or chuck, cut into very small pieces
> as an alternative, you can use:
>> 2 pounds ground beef
>> 1/2 pound ground veal
>> 1/2 pound ground pork
> or
>> 3 pounds ground chicken, dark meat

THE SPICES

> 4 tablespoons ancho chili powder
> 4 tablespoons cumin
> 1 tablespoon garlic powder
> salt and pepper

THE REST

> 2 large sweet onions
> 4–5 peppers, combine red, yellow and orange bell peppers, stemmed, seeded and diced small (I cut out the thin inner white membrane before chopping.)
> 2 jalapeño peppers, chopped
> 2 serrano chilis, chopped fine
> 3 stalks of celery, chopped
> 1 large can tomatoes or 4–5 fresh, chopped
> 5–6 cups beef stock
> 3 cans any type of beans or 3 cups cooked fresh beans, drained and rinsed

1. In a very large-bottom pot, brown meat with a little oil, seasoning with half of the spice mixture. Remove meat and place in a bowl to hold.

2. In the same pan, sauté all the vegetables except the tomatoes, seasoning with the rest of the spice mixture.

3. Return meat to pan; add the tomatoes and beef stock. Simmer about 10 minutes.

4. Add the beans and continue simmering about 30 minutes to an hour. Adjust seasoning as you go. The longer you cook this the better.

Jewels' favorite fixin's are *cotija* cheese, green onions and sour cream.

JEWELS' SMART IDEA

Chili is something you can do ahead of time and it only gets better the next day. I am not big on keeping things in the freezer for more than a week or two, but it's not a bad idea to store a little chili there to pull out in a pinch!

jewels' delicioso arróz con pollo

JEWELS SAYS • This dish demonstrates how I can get inspired by crockery or cookware! A beautiful, huge paella pan is perfect for "family-style eating" and a really great way to change something basic into something very interesting. My version of this classic Cuban dish takes just a few ingredients to prepare. When served in the pan, this simple meal of chicken and rice becomes a feast for the eyes and the belly! Pair it with a beautiful salad and you can feel good about feeding your friends and family a healthy, comforting and sophisticated meal.

SERVES 8–10.

> 2 whole chickens, each cut into 10 pieces
> (the whole breast cut into 4 pieces)
> salt and pepper
> cumin
> paprika
> oil, for browning
> 1 onion, diced
> 2 shallots, diced
> 2 cloves garlic, diced
> 3 cups brown kalijira rice (You can use any rice, but may have to
> adjust liquid and cooking time. White rice needs less liquid
> and cooks faster than brown.)
> 6–8 cups chicken stock
> small handful parsley, finely chopped

1. Season the chicken pieces with salt, pepper, cumin and paprika.

2. Heat the pan. Because of its size you may have to use high heat or 2 burners, moving the pan about to distribute the heat evenly. Use a few glugs of oil to just brown the chicken on both sides, skin side first.

3. Take the chicken out and set it aside. Add the onion, shallots, garlic and rice and sauté for a moment. Then add the stock and stir, making sure to scrape up all the good bits from the bottom of the pan.

4. Place the chicken in the pan, skin side up, and cover with a lid or foil.

5. You can either continue simmering on the stove top or place the chicken in the oven at 375 degrees F to complete cooking. Cook about 1 hour or until the chicken and rice are completely cooked. Check the liquid from time to time; you may need to add a little more stock, depending on which kind of rice you have used. When you do, pour some of the juices over the chicken to moisten.

6. After removing from the oven, let the chicken sit for a few minutes. Sprinkle parsley over the top.

JEWELS' SMART IDEA

You can make this dish in any pan—or several pans—but if you invest in a large paella pan, it will inspire you to make this and so many other dishes. Ask your butcher to chop up your chicken for you!

so amazing armenian lula kebobs

JILL SAYS • My best friend, Karrie, is half Armenian. I met her in the sixth grade and, as a kid, always loved eating at her house, where I was introduced to all kinds of new delicious dishes. These tasty lula kebobs were, and still are, one of my favorites. They are the perfect marriage between a meat patty and a kebob. If you don't have skewers, you can form the meat into patties or even meatballs.

SERVES 8–10.

  3 pounds ground sirloin or lamb

  1 large yellow onion, finely chopped

  1/4 cup parsley, finely chopped

  1 tablespoon fresh mint, finely chopped

  1 egg

  2 teaspoons ground cumin

  1 tablespoon paprika

  1/2 teaspoon garlic powder

  2 teaspoons salt

  1 teaspoon freshly ground pepper

  2 tablespoons tomato paste

  juice of 1/2 lemon

1. Use your hands to mix the ingredients together until just combined. Overmixing may result in meat that is tough.

2. Still using your hands, gently squeeze the meat onto metal skewers to form kebobs. Place the kebobs on a sheet tray lined with parchment. If you have time, it's a good idea to cover the tray with plastic and place the kebobs in the fridge for 30 minutes or so. There are two reasons for this: The flavors have a chance to meld together, and the cold keeps the meat from falling off the skewers.

3. Heat the grill. Once hot, grill the kebobs about 3–4 minutes on each side. Serve with *Parsley Is the Key to Success Salad* (page 95) and *Sumac-Flavored Red Onions* (page 221).

flap meat is cheap!

JEWELS SAYS • It is amazing what you can learn from your butcher if you take the time to ask a few questions. I planned to prepare a fajita-style meal one day and did not see any skirt or flank steak, which were my usual picks. When I asked for them, my butcher suggested that I try "flap meat," a cut I hadn't heard of before. I took his suggestion, and when I grilled it, the texture and flavor were much better than the other cuts of meat. Flap meat, also known as "bavette," is a much more tender cut that is perfect for the raw flame! Because it is thin, it needs only moments over very hot coals and is best served medium rare. Like the other cuts, it is important to slice this meat against the grain in thin strips.

Jill and I now choose flap meat to serve at our big family gatherings. Anyone can grill it. It's quick to prepare and won't break the bank!

SERVES 10–12.

> **12 pieces of flap meat**
> **2 onions, minced**
> **3 cloves of garlic, crushed**
> **a bunch of cilantro, tear off stems and chop to use in marinade,**
> **   reserving leaves for garnish**
> **cumin**
> **garlic powder**
> **salt and pepper**
> **a few big glugs of olive oil**

1. Combine all the ingredients and rub on the meat. Let sit for a while.

2. Grill over an open flame until medium rare. Allow the meat to rest for a few moments before slicing against the grain into thin strips.

This dish can be served with tortillas as a taco meat or on top of a salad. You can also toss the meat in a little *Grilled-Tomato Puree* (page 119) and sprinkle with reserved cilantro and lime for an extra layer of fresh flavor!

JEWELS' SMART IDEA

You can use this leftover meat for *Smart Idea Burritos* (page 187) or *Delicious, Clean and Healthy Tostada* (page 83).

achiote-marinated pork tenderloin

JILL SAYS • Achiote paste, a Mexican ingredient that comes in a block, is made with vinegar, salt, garlic and annatto seeds. Its super-unique flavor is wonderful with chicken, beef or pork tenderloin, which doesn't take long to cook.

SERVES 10–12.

> 1 recipe *Achiote Marinade* (page 85)
> ¼ cup orange juice
> 2 tablespoons brown sugar
> 4 pork tenderloins
> tortillas

1. Prepare the *Achiote Marinade* and add the orange juice and brown sugar.

2. Put the pork tenderloins in an extra-large Ziploc bag and pour the marinade inside. Close the bag tight and move the meat around to completely coat with the marinade. Refrigerate 1–4 hours or overnight.

3. Preheat oven to 400 degrees F. Heat a large, heavy skillet over high heat. When the pan is practically smoking, add two of the pork tenderloins and brown on all sides. Remove from the pan and transfer to a sheet tray. Repeat with remaining two tenderloins. You can also brown this on the barbecue.

4. Finish cooking tenderloins in the oven another 10–15 minutes.

5. While the pork is in the oven, heat the tortillas on a warm pan on the stove.

6. When the pork is done, slice and serve with *Red Cabbage Coleslaw* (page 285), *Mashed Yams* (page 281) and/or *Guacamole* (page 63) and *Salsa* (page 62) and black beans.

JILL'S SMART IDEA

se any leftover pork tenderloin to make *Smart Idea Burritos* (page 187)

moroccan spiced lamb and veggie stew

JEWELS SAYS • I strongly believe that when you travel to other countries, it expands your heart, soul, mind and, of course, your palate. You can expose your family to different corners of the world when you cook food from other cultures together.

My friend Inna took me on a trip that changed my life. We went to Morocco, where I was able to experience for myself the sights, smells and tastes of this amazing North African culture. I was so impressed by the creativity of the Moroccans. The highlight of my trip was learning how to cook in classic Moroccan *tagines*, pyramid-shaped clay ovens for just one person. I savored *tagine*-cooked vegetables and lamb dishes. They came out so tender and beautiful, seasoned with amazingly aromatic spices. I came home and began making Moroccan food at work and for my own family. The dishes stimulated conversations and opened people's minds to the different ways that people choose to live. I want my family to know about people from other lands and cultures. In some small way I want to lead them to a greater understanding of different beliefs and lifestyles. So I do what I can—by cooking!

SERVES 10–12.

oil, for browning

3 pounds leg of lamb, deboned, cut into medium chunks and generously seasoned with salt, pepper and half of the following spice mix:

2 tablespoons ground coriander

2 tablespoons ground cumin

2 tablespoons turmeric

2 small onions, diced

2 cloves garlic, smashed and chopped

a few saffron threads

1 small can crushed tomatoes (I use San Marzano)

a handful of cilantro stems and parsley stems, tied with string or in cheesecloth

4 cups chicken broth or stock

1 bay leaf

2 potatoes

3 zucchini, cut in chunks

1/2 butternut squash, cut in chunks

salt, to taste

1. In a large, heavy-bottomed shallow pot, heat a little oil and begin browning the seasoned lamb.

2. Add the onions, garlic and saffron threads and continue cooking, making sure to scrape the bits from the bottom of the pan.

3. Add the tomatoes, cilantro and parsley stems, chicken broth and bay leaf. Simmer until meat begins to tenderize.

4. Add the potatoes, zucchini and squash and check to see if you need to add more stock. Cook until the meat and vegetables are soft and tender, and most of the liquid is absorbed.

5. Add salt, to taste.

Serve in a *tagine* and eat Morrocan-style!

sumac-flavored red onions

Sumac is a wonderfully tart spice used in Middle Eastern cooking. These onions are great with lula kebobs, a piece of steak, a lamb chop or even with fish or chicken.

1 large red onion, cut in half and thinly sliced

1 tablespoon sumac

Mix the onion and sumac together and let sit for about 10 minutes before serving.

JILL'S SMART IDEA

Once my mother-in-law, Lynn, made a shepherd's pie out of this recipe. She started by sautéing onions and tomatoes. Next she broke up the cooked meat, added it to some veggies, put mashed potatoes and cheese on top and baked it. Delicious!

refreshing thai fish

JEWELS SAYS • The bright flavors of Thai food are some of the easiest to introduce to your friends and family. This parchment paper–wrapped fish is so simple, one of your kitchen helpers could put them together! The fun part about this is the shopping at the Thai market for the galangal root, but if this is not possible, use ginger root instead. The parchment seals in and infuses the flavors and the dish takes just minutes to cook! I serve the fish right in the paper and let everyone open up their own beautifully scented packages.

SERVES 8–10.

> 8 very fresh pieces of snapper (you can use flounder or sole as well),
>   seasoned with salt and pepper
> 8 large pieces parchment paper
> 2 leeks, thinly sliced
> 16 very thin slices of galangal root (or ginger)
> 2 stalks lemongrass, tender inside section only, sliced thinly on the bias
> 16 big pieces of Thai basil sprigs (or use any fresh basil), 8 to cook and 8 to garnish
> a beautiful, fruity extra-virgin olive oil
> salt

1. Lay one piece of snapper in the center of a sheet of parchment paper. Top with some of the leek, two slices of galangal, some of the lemongrass, and one basil leaf. Drizzle with a little olive oil and sprinkle with a little salt.

2. Bring the longer edges of the parchment together; fold the paper down several times until tight. Twist the edges and tuck underneath to seal in juices. Place on a sheet pan and repeat with the other five pieces of fish.

3. Cook for 8–10 minutes at 425 degrees F, depending on the thickness of the fish.

4. Place garnish of Thai basil on top of fish itself (if serving out of the paper package) or on top of the closed package and enjoy!

JEWELS' SMART IDEA

If you don't want to wrap the individual pieces, you can also use a full side of halibut or any other fish. Place the whole side of fish in one large piece of parchment. Wrap and cook just a few minutes longer.

quick meat sauce

JEWELS SAYS • This sauce is made with the meat mixture from the *Turkey Patties for Manly Men* (page 177) and the *Beautiful, Clean Albondigas Soup* (page 125). Having the mixture ready to go is a great way to get a head start on dinner!

MAKES 8–10 CUPS.

2–3 cups (approximately) of *Meatball Mixture* (page 125)

a glug of olive oil

2 small onions, chopped

2 cloves garlic, smashed and chopped

a pinch of crushed red pepper

2 large cans crushed tomatoes

a pinch of sugar

a pinch of oregano

a few dashes of salt

1 bay leaf

1. In a heavy pot, brown the meat in olive oil, breaking it up as you do. Remove the meat and set aside.

2. In the same pan, sauté the onions, garlic and red pepper until the onions are translucent.

3. Add the tomatoes, sugar, oregano, salt and bay leaf. Simmer for 1/2 hour or longer, stirring often. Remove the bay leaf.

JEWELS' SMART IDEA

ake extra to store in the freezer.

chicken-lettuce cups

JILL SAYS • This recipe is inspired by my friend Molly. She loves my *Chicken Potstickers* (page 237). One day while making them at home, she realized she was out of gyoza skins, so she cooked the meat and put it in lettuce cups instead. Now she eats these lettuce cups all the time. They make a great dinner that is light and healthy.

SERVES 8–10.

THE FILLING

2 tablespoons peanut oil

2 teaspoons sesame oil

24 shitake mushrooms, finely chopped

2 large carrots, peeled and very finely chopped

4 scallions, very finely chopped

2 teaspoons minced ginger

1 teaspoon minced garlic

2 pounds ground white meat chicken (or combination of white and dark)

$1/2$ teaspoon freshly ground pepper

2 small cans of water chestnuts, drained and finely diced

THE SAUCE

1 cup soy sauce

4 tablespoons seasoned rice wine vinegar

4 tablespoons orange juice

4 tablespoons brown sugar

4 tablespoons water

3 tablespoons cornstarch

1 teaspoon chili flakes

4 tablespoons oyster sauce

THE LETTUCE CUPS

2 heads of iceberg lettuce, washed and leaves peeled for lettuce cups

1. For the sauce, mix all ingredients together with a whisk or shake together in a jar. Set aside.

2. Heat a large nonstick skillet over medium-high heat. When the pan is hot, add the peanut and sesame oils. Sauté the mushrooms, carrots, scallions, ginger and garlic for 4–5 minutes until the mushrooms are cooked and the vegetables are soft.

3. Add the chicken and cook. Stir constantly, breaking up the meat.

4. When the chicken is almost cooked, add the pepper and the sauce, bring to a boil, reduce heat to simmer and continue cooking 5–6 minutes.

5. While the chicken is cooking, prepare the lettuce cups.

6. Remove pan from heat, stir in water chestnuts, spoon the mixture into lettuce cups and serve.

JILL'S SMART IDEA

To simplify your shopping, note that the ingredients for this recipe are almost exactly the same as the *Chicken Potstickers* recipe (page 237).

healthy babies, healthy kids

JILL SAYS • My baby, Charlie, is definitely his mother's son. From the time he was five or six months old, he's always wanted to eat whatever we were eating. On our first trip to Australia with our baby, Simon and I were enjoying a dinner of sweet potatoes and lamb, a typical Aussie meal. Charlie was far too young to share food directly off our plates, but that didn't matter to him. He wailed and cried until I broke down and put a bit of our meal in a blender. Spooning it into a baby mesh feeder, I gave it to him to suck on. He was in seventh heaven. You wouldn't believe how much of that food he managed to suction straight through the mesh.

We all want our kids to be healthy. Since becoming a mom, I'm more conscious of eating healthfully myself because Charlie pays such close attention to everything I eat. It is so clear to me that I need to set a good example. If there is something on my plate I would not give him, I have to ask myself why. Maybe I shouldn't be eating it either.

Our mom did an amazing job of giving us the healthiest food when we were young. While other kids got pb&j on Wonder bread in their lunch boxes, we opened ours to find freshly roasted turkey, beautifully sliced over julienned vegetables and butter lettuce, with a hard-boiled egg sliced and arranged like a Japanese fan on top. Her tuna sandwiches were so good that other kids tried to bribe us to get them or to buy our lunches off us outright!

Even when kids are very young, we believe in exposing them to a wide variety of foods, always assuming they might like something—even if we don't. Before turning one, Charlie was already eating lentils, avocados, cheese, fish, all kinds of fruits and vegetables and lamb chops. The kids I know love the recipes in this chapter. All kids are different, of course, so when preparing their meals for them, keep an open mind. Be persistent about getting them to taste things, even if they have tried them before and think they don't like them. We believe in trying again and again. Their taste buds do change, just like ours. When I was a picky little kid, I only liked a handful of things. But my parents' subtle persistence paid off. Now there is almost nothing I won't eat.

healthy babies, healthy kids,

unfried chicken tenders—a sure bet

JILL SAYS • What kid doesn't love chicken tenders? This is a very simple recipe. I use a combination of bread crumbs and cornflake crumbs for flavor and crunch.

SERVES 4–6.

16 chicken tenders
salt and pepper, to taste
1 egg, beaten
1/4 cup milk
1/2 cup bread crumbs
1/2 cup cornflake crumbs
organic olive oil spray

1. Preheat oven to 375 degrees F. Season chicken with salt and pepper and let sit for couple of minutes.

2. In a medium-sized mixing bowl, whisk the egg and milk and add the chicken tenders.

3. In a shallow dish, mix together the bread crumbs and cornflake crumbs. Season with salt and pepper.

4. Dip each chicken tender on both sides into the crumb mixture. Place on a sheet tray sprayed with olive oil. When finished breading, spray tenders with olive oil and bake in the oven 10–12 minutes. You can also sauté tenders quickly. Either way, they will be a healthy hit with your kids!

JILL'S SMART IDEA

You can make these ahead of time, freeze them, pull them out and then reheat them in the oven in no time. I also keep the seasoned cornflake-bread-crumb mixture in an airtight container in the pantry, ready to use.

"My doctor told me to stop havng intimate dinners for four—unless there are three other people."

—Orson Welles

nana's fideo and chicken soup

JILL SAYS • Fideos are thin noodles, almost like angel hair pasta packaged as little round nests of noodles. As kids, we loved eating this soup and we still do. It's a favorite with all of the kids in our family. Because the flavors in the soup are so mellow, even the youngest of eaters will enjoy this. It requires very few ingredients and little time to prepare.

SERVES 4–6.

> 2 tablespoons olive oil or vegetable oil
> 4 nests of fideo noodles (about $1/2$ package)
> $1/2$ medium onion, diced very small
> $1/2$ cup tomato sauce
> 6 cups chicken broth, vegetable broth or water
> $1/4$ teaspoon garlic powder
> salt and pepper, to taste
> 1 cup chicken, cooked and shredded into small pieces

1. Heat a medium-sized pot on the stove over medium-high heat. When the pan is hot, add the oil and, using your hands, break up and add the noodles. Stirring constantly, cook noodles until brown and toasty.

2. Next add the chopped onions and sauté for a couple more minutes. Add the tomato sauce and stir for a minute more.

3. Add the chicken broth, garlic powder and salt and pepper. Bring to a boil, reduce heat to low and continue simmering until the noodles are soft, about 15 minutes.

4. Now stir in the chicken and cook for a couple more minutes, just until the chicken is warm. Serve hot.

chicken potstickers

JILL SAYS • A few of these delicious potstickers served with some edamame and rice make a great meal for kids and adults alike.

SERVES 4–6.

THE POTSTICKERS

    1 tablespoon peanut oil, plus additional oil to sauté potstickers

    1 teaspoon sesame oil

    1 large carrot, peeled and very finely chopped

    2 scallions, very finely chopped

    1 teaspoon ginger, minced

    1/2 teaspoon garlic, minced

    1 pound ground white-meat chicken (or a combination of white and dark meat chicken)

    2 tablespoons soy sauce

    1 egg

    1/2 teaspoon freshly ground pepper

    egg wash (1 egg, beaten with 2 tablespoons water)

    2 tablespoons cornstarch

    1 package gyoza skins (or use round wonton wrappers, available in the refrigerated section of many grocery stores)

THE SOY GLAZE

    1/2 cup soy sauce

    2 tablespoons seasoned rice wine vinegar

    2 tablespoons orange juice

    2 tablespoons brown sugar

    2 tablespoons water

    1/2 teaspoon chili flakes

1. Prepare the soy glaze by mixing all ingredients together. Set aside.

2. Place a medium-sized nonstick skillet over medium-high heat. When the pan is hot, add the peanut and sesame oils. Now sauté the carrot, scallions, ginger and garlic, 2–3 minutes, just until the carrots are slightly soft. Remove the pan from heat and let the vegetables cool.

3. Place the ground chicken in a mixing bowl. Add sautéed carrots, soy sauce, egg (not the egg wash) and ground pepper. Mix until well combined, cover with plastic wrap and let stand in the fridge 30 minutes (not absolutely necessary, but it gives the flavors a chance to meld together).

4. Prepare the egg wash.

5. Line a sheet tray with parchment and sprinkle with cornstarch.

6. Making sure your work surface is dry, lay out 12 gyoza skins. Brush lightly with the egg wash and spoon a large teaspoon full of chicken mixture in the center. Fold the wontons in half to form a half-moon and pinch closed with your fingers. Continue this process until you have used all of the mixture. Lay the uncooked potstickers on the parchment-lined tray. Keep in the refrigerator until ready to cook. At this point, you may freeze the potstickers and cook at another time. (If frozen, let defrost slightly before you continue to the next step.)

7. Heat a medium-sized nonstick skillet over medium-high heat. When the pan is hot, add a couple tablespoons of peanut oil and sauté potstickers until brown and crispy, 2–3 minutes. Then flip them over and continue cooking until crispy on both sides. Remove any excess oil from the pan.

8. With the potstickers still in the pan, add a small ladle full of the sauce and cook until potstickers are nicely coated with the sauce, approximately 1–2 minutes.

JILL'S SMART IDEA

Freeze some of the uncooked potstickers and make *Wonton Soup* (page 127) another night. Try making *Chicken-Lettuce Cups* (page 225), using almost the same ingredients.

sweet chicken sushi with brown rice

JILL SAYS • Since sushi has become so popular among adults, it is now becoming a trend among teens and younger kids as well. Making sushi is a lot of fun, so it will be easy to get your kids involved in preparing this recipe.

SERVES 4–6.

    6 boneless, skinless chicken thighs (or 4 chicken breasts)

    1/2 cup Asian sweet chili sauce

    1/2 teaspoon salt

    1 cup cooked brown rice, at room temperature

    4 sheets nori paper

1. In medium-sized mixing bowl, stir together the chicken, sweet chili sauce and salt. Cover with plastic and refrigerate for a few hours or overnight.

2. Heat a grill or broiler and cook the chicken, turning once halfway through (about 5–6 minutes on each side). Allow to cool a little and slice into long pieces.

3. Place a sheet of nori on a sushi roller and spread about 1/4 cup of brown rice on top of it. Place a few chicken slices on the rice and roll. Cut into pieces and serve.

JILL'S SMART IDEA

Buy the nori in small packages instead of in bulk so that they stay crispy and fresh. When you do store them, make sure you store them in an airtight Ziploc bag. If you don't have nori, you can make a chicken-and-rice bowl, which kids love!

organic apple and prune sauce

JILL SAYS • I love making food for my baby. Giving him the healthiest food possible (which makes me feel like Supermom) is the main advantage. Another is that I can add variety to his diet and change the consistency of the foods he eats.

MAKES 3–4 CUPS.

6 organic Fuji apples, peeled and cut into small chunks
8 organic pitted prunes
1/4 cup water
a pinch of cinnamon

1. In a medium-sized pan, mix all the ingredients together and slowly bring to a boil. Continue to mix occasionally, reduce heat to simmer and cook partially covered 20–30 minutes.

2. Use a blender or food processor to puree. For tiny babies, push cooled mixture through a sieve to make it extra smooth. For older babies, use a potato masher instead of blending for a chunkier consistency.

JILL'S SMART IDEA

As kids get older, instead of making smooth purees, I leave the food a little chunkier to suit their growing needs. Also, for grown-ups, this puree can be stirred into oatmeal for a yummy and healthy breakfast!

super food for babies

JEWELS SAYS • Combining yummy vegetables with quinoa, which is both a protein and a grain, makes this baby food amazing. Quinoa is full of protein, calcium, iron and several B vitamins, in addition to an almost perfect balance of all amino acids (so important for little growing bodies). Amazingly, half a cup of quinoa will provide a small child's protein needs for the day. I feel so good about feeding this super food to my baby, Austin.

MAKES APPROXIMATELY 6 CUPS.

 1/4 cup quinoa, rinsed

 1 cup broccoli, cut in medium-sized pieces

 1 cup zucchini, cut in chunks

 a small handful of parsley

 4 cups organic low-sodium chicken stock or water

1. In a medium-sized pan, mix all the ingredients together and slowly bring to a boil. Reduce the heat to simmer and cook partially covered 30–40 minutes.

2. Puree in a blender or food processor. For tiny babies, pass the mixture through a sieve to be sure it is extra smooth. For older babies, depending on their age and development, leave it chunkier, instead of blending.

red lentil and veggie puree

JILL SAYS • I made this puree the first time because a couple of yellow zucchini from the farmers' market were too gorgeous to pass up. At home, I combined the zucchini with crimson lentils. Charlie loved it. And now I make it all the time.

MAKES APPROXIMATELY 6 CUPS.

> 2 yellow zucchini, cut in medium-sized chunks
> 2 carrots, peeled and cut into medium-sized chunks
> 3/4 cup cauliflower, cut into medium-sized pieces
> 1/2 cup crimson or red lentils
> 4–5 cups organic low-sodium chicken stock or water

1. In a medium-sized pan, mix all ingredients together and slowly bring to a boil. Reduce heat to simmer and cook partially covered 30–40 minutes.

2. Puree in a blender or food processor. For tiny babies, pass mixture through a sieve to be sure it is extra smooth. For older babies, depending on their age and development, leave a little chunkier, instead of blending.

JILL'S SMART IDEA

Thin out this puree or the one above *(Super Food for Babies)* with a little stock and add some fresh herbs to make a delicious soup for grown-ups!

when friends and family come over for dinner

JEWELS SAYS • When Kiko and I first started dating, we were just having fun and not thinking about long-term commitment. Kiko had been a bachelor for a very (very!) long time—forty-eight years to be exact—and saw no reason that this should change. I was recently divorced and going out on a lot of first dates. Kiko's friends—on the other hand—quickly hatched their own ideas about us. One night, three couples—a lawyer, a judge, an entrepreneur and their amazing wives—came over for dinner. There are special occasions in life that make every Family Chef want to pull out the good china, use the best tablecloth and spend all day preparing a meal. This was one of those nights. I made two of my favorite dishes: *Light Curry Lobster Tails* and *Thai Beef Salad* (recipes below).

The evening seemed to set Kiko's friends on a campaign. They began urging us to get married. This trio of happily married couples made a strong case that we should do as they had. I think they really got Kiko thinking about it seriously—his friends, that is, and his stomach!

The recipes in this chapter are perfect for special occasions. Their preparation may take a little more time and money, but the results will be well worth the effort!

You'll notice more detailed techniques and unique ingredients. Because they are more complex, these are my favorite recipes. I live for those times when I can invest hours in preparing a single dish. Don't be intimidated by these recipes; just try one of them. If you can invest a little time, you'll see they are much easier than you think.

when friends and family come over for dinner

perfect-meld-of-flavors thai beef salad

JEWELS SAYS • When you are a chef, people expect to come to your home and be completely blown away by your food. This can be intimidating, even for the best of cooks! But I've got a secret weapon that works every time: my Thai beef salad. This mouthwatering salad has no peer. The deeply flavorful beef sets up behind a light, fresh salad made with lime, mint, basil and cilantro. I love to make it with friends and teach it at cooking parties. Many of the steps can be performed simultaneously. When you put it all together, the result is nothing short of impressive.

SERVES 6.

THE MEAT

2$\frac{1}{2}$ **pounds fillet or steak of your choice**

THE MARINADE

(If you do not have a particular ingredient, just use what you have!)

1 shallot, chopped

2 cloves of garlic, smashed

$\frac{1}{4}$ cup brown sugar

$\frac{1}{2}$″ piece ginger, smashed

$\frac{1}{2}$ stalk lemongrass, middle part only, crushed and chopped

2 teaspoons sriracha (hot chili sauce)

$\frac{1}{4}$ cup soy sauce

$\frac{1}{4}$ cup Asian sesame seed oil

$\frac{1}{2}$ lime, juiced

$\frac{1}{8}$ cup coconut vinegar

THE SALAD

1 head butter lettuce, torn in small pieces

1 head red-leaf lettuce, torn in small pieces

3 big handfuls tender pea shoots

$\frac{1}{2}$ bunch basil leaves, torn into small pieces (lemon basil works well, too)

1 bunch mint leaves, torn into pieces

$\frac{1}{2}$ bunch cilantro, rough chopped or torn

THE DRESSING

$\frac{1}{4}$ cup coconut vinegar

1 lime, juiced

2 teaspoons fish sauce

1 tablespoon palm sugar or regular sugar

¼ cup roasted peanut oil

a small handful Thai chilis, cut into thin rounds

a splash extra-virgin olive oil

a dash fleur de sel (salt)

a few cranks of the pepper mill

1. If you choose to make the *Crispy Shallots* (recipe below), fry them and set aside.

2. Make the marinade: Put all ingredients in a blender to puree into chunky liquid.

3. Pour the marinade over the meat. Rub in well and let sit for about 15 minutes.

4. While the meat is marinating, make the salad dressing: Put all ingredients in a bowl or jar and mix. *Do not use a blender.* Set aside.

5. Mix the salad greens, put in a bowl and cover with a damp paper towel.

6. Grill the meat and let rest for 5 minutes. While it is resting, dress the salad.

7. Slice the meat into thin strips, against the grain of the meat, and fan on the side of the salad. Sprinkle the crispy shallots (if using) over the salad and serve.

the crispy shallots (optional)

3 cups peanut oil, for frying

15 shallots, peeled and sliced in thin rounds

salt, to taste

1. In a medium-sized pan, heat oil until shallot rings bubble when you drop them in. This is not a *fast* deep fry, but a 25-minute process. The shallots turn golden and sweet as they cook.

2. Season each batch with salt. Let cool and store in an airtight container.

JEWELS' SMART IDEA

Make the beef marinade, the salad dressing and the crispy shallots as much as a day ahead to save time.

"Dining with one's friends and beloved family is certainly one of life's primal and most innocent delights, one that is soul-satisfying and eternal."

—Julia Child

light curry lobster tails (or shrimp)

JEWELS SAYS • My close friend West and I cannot account for the intense love we have for each other because we're *such* completely different people. We both felt it the moment we met, before either had spoken. It was a friendship *coup de foudre*. We also both love Hawaii—I mean, *love* those islands—and share the same aching-heart desire to be a part of the Hawaiian culture. It's the only way we can explain our super-strong connection: We figure we must have shared a past life as Pacific islanders.

We haven't gone to Hawaii together yet in this life. But we have made this luscious dish for friends here on the beach in California with real aloha spirit. We still talk about the way our friends devoured multiple platefuls of everything we served them and had such a great time.

This dish has a few special ingredients, including turmeric and lemongrass, that are worth the trip to a specialty market or buying online. But, if you can't find them fresh, you can certainly use the powdered versions as well. These spices have an exotic flavor that you and your guests will come to crave.

SERVES 6–8.

the marinade

a big handful of cumin seeds, lightly toasted in a dry pan,
    then ground fine (You can use a clean coffee grinder.)

about 2 inches fresh ginger, peeled and chopped

about 2 inches peeled fresh turmeric or 1½ tablespoons dry turmeric

2 shallots, roughly chopped

2 cloves garlic, roughly chopped

2–3 stalks lemongrass, tender center only, chopped fine

zest and juice of 1 lime

1 heaping tablespoon palm sugar (or ½ teaspoon white sugar
    and ½ teaspoon brown sugar)

½ tablespoon salt

about ½ cup extra-virgin olive oil

OPTIONAL ADDITIONS:

¼ pound butter, cold and cut in pieces

2 kaffir lime leaves, sliced into very thin strips

Combine all the ingredients (except the butter and the lime leaves) in a blender, mixing until you achieve a smooth paste. If you are using the butter, incorporate small pieces at a time, while the blender is running on low. Stir in lime leaves (if using). Set aside. Can be made a day in advance.

the lobster

6 whole lobsters

1. Blanch the lobster: Fill a large pot (that can fit one lobster) with water and a small handful of salt and bring to a boil. (You only need enough water to cover one lobster.)

2. Get a bowl of ice water ready and set aside.

3. When the water is at a full boil, plunge one lobster into the water for about 2 minutes, remove, then plunge immediately into the ice water. (I use a cooler filled with ice water when I am doing a lot of these.) Repeat with all five lobsters.

4. Remove the lobsters from ice water when cooled. Remove each tail by twisting from the body. (Twist off the claws, too. You can use these later.) Cut the tails in half, through the shell and down the center with a very sharp knife. You can do this ahead of time and store in the fridge until ready to grill.

5. Rub a generous amount of the marinade on the lobster tails, pouring a bit in between the shell and flesh, being careful not to separate them.

6. Let them sit for at least 5 or 10 minutes.

7. Grill the lobster tails, flesh side down first, turning frequently and brushing with a bit of the extra marinade. They should be done in about 8–12 minutes.

8. Serve warm. I like to serve them with forbidden rice (page 301).

JILL'S SMART IDEA

I love to make this with shrimp to save both time and money!

filo crisps with morel mushrooms

JEWELS SAYS • This dish is very different from most in this book, but I had to include it in this section that gives us a chance to "fancy it up." I would not advocate eating these on a regular basis but these decadent little crisps are a tasty treat on a special occasion.

Filo dough may sound intimidating, but honestly, I am not a baker, and if I can make them, so can you. I like to follow Jill to the Greek market (she's a regular) and buy the filo fresh, but you can get it frozen at most any supermarket. I use the normal and not "superthin" version. Filo usually comes in a kind of "folded roll," so unroll it and lay it out on the counter covered with a lightly damp paper towel. If the dough hits the air, it will immediately dry out and crumble, so keep it covered the entire time you are working on it.

If morel mushrooms are not in season, you can use shitakes or even brown mushrooms, but be sure to cut them thinly so that they lie flat under the filo. You can also omit the mushrooms and just use herbs and a bit of cheese.

SERVES 6–8.

THE FILLING

  a few glugs of olive oil

  a little pat of butter

  3 big handfuls of morel mushrooms, stems cut off, cut in rings, rinsed and dried on a
      paper towel

  $3/4$ of a shallot, chopped fine

  salt and pepper

  a small handful of thyme leaves, lightly chopped

  1 sage leaf, chopped up fine

  about $1/2$ cup of grated or crumbled *cotija* cheese (you can use Parmesan or Pecorino
      Romano instead)

  $1/2$ bunch of parsley, leaves only

THE FILO

  $1/2$ pound of unsalted butter

  1 box of filo dough (thawed if frozen)

1. Preheat oven to 375 degrees F and set aside two baking sheets with a Silpat (optional).

2. Prepare the filling: Using the olive oil and butter, sauté the mushrooms with the shallot. While cooking, season with salt and pepper and add the thyme and sage leaf. Cook until the liquid is absorbed and the mushrooms are a little crispy and dried. Set aside to cool.

3. Get the *cotija* cheese and the parsley ready in two separate bowls.

4. Prepare the filo: Melt the butter and keep nearby. Peel off one sheet of the filo and lay it flat on the dry counter. Quickly and lightly butter with a pastry brush. Sprinkle one-eighth of the cheese over the buttered sheet.

5. Peel off a second sheet of filo, lay on top of the first sheet and brush with butter. Sprinkle another eighth of the cheese over the buttered sheet.

6. Add sheet number 3 of filo on top of the first two, brush lightly with butter and sprinkle another eighth of the cheese.

7. Scatter half of the sautéed mushrooms over the cheese.

8. Add a fourth sheet, brush with lightly with butter, sprinkle another eighth of the cheese and add half of the parsley leaves.

9. Top with the final sheet of filo and brush with butter.

10. Cut the large rectangle of 5-layered filo into 6 squares or long triangles. Place them on the baking sheet butter side down, leaving a little space in between the pieces.

11. Bake the filo for about 10–12 minutes or until lightly brown, being careful not to darken them too much as it will change the taste.

12. Repeat to make another batch.

13. Let the crisps cool slightly before serving.

do-it-ahead chicken chiles rellenos

JILL SAYS • If you like to get as much food prep done as possible before your guests arrive, this is the perfect recipe for you. You can make these chiles rellenos the day before and store them on a sheet tray tightly covered with plastic wrap. When your guests arrive, just remove the plastic and pop them in the oven. They are tasty and filling—a healthy, satisfying alternative to the traditional fried chiles rellenos. I serve these rellenos with black beans, salsa and guacamole.

SERVES 8–10.

- 8 chicken breast halves (or 4 whole breasts), bone in and skin on
- salt and pepper
- 10–12 fresh poblano chilis
- 1 small yellow onion, finely diced
- $1/2$ cup cilantro, roughly chopped
- 3–4 ears of corn, kernels removed
- $1^1/2$ cup *Tomatillo Sauce* (recipe below) or use good-quality canned tomatillo sauce
- 4 cups grated cheese, mixture of cheddar, jack and *cotija*

1. Preheat oven to 400 degrees F. Season chicken on both sides with salt and pepper. Roast chicken in oven for 45–50 minutes.

2. While the chicken is roasting, roast and peel the poblano chilis. Cut a slit in each of the chilis and remove seeds. Set aside.

3. Once the chicken is roasted, let it cool slightly and, using your hands, shred it into pieces. Place in a large mixing bowl.

4. To the chicken, add the onion, cilantro, shaved corn, *Tomatillo Sauce* and $2^1/2$ cups of grated cheese, salt and pepper. Using a wooden spoon, or your hands, mix ingredients together. Taste and adjust seasoning by adding more salt or pepper, if necessary.

5. Stuff the roasted chilis with the chicken mixture and top with remaining $1^1/2$ cups of grated cheese. Put finished chilis on a sheet tray. If you are doing this the day ahead, cover tightly with plastic wrap and store in the fridge.

6. Bake at 350 degrees F for 20–30 minutes, until the chilis are hot and the cheese on top has melted. If you made them the day ahead, allow more cooking time in the oven or take them out of the fridge and let them come to room temp, before putting them in the oven.

tomatillo sauce

10 medium tomatillos, husked and rinsed several times

¹/₂ medium onion, finely diced

1 tablespoon olive oil

1 small clove of garlic, minced

a handful of cilantro, roughly chopped

1 chicken bouillon cube

salt, to taste

1. Bring a medium-sized pot of water to boil. When the water boils, add the tomatillos and cook them until translucent, about 4–5 minutes. Drain the tomatillos and puree in a blender or food processor. Set aside.

2. Return the empty pot to the stove over medium-high heat. Sauté the onions in olive oil for 2–3 minutes. Add the garlic and cilantro and sauté another minute or two.

3. Place blended tomatillos back in pan, along with the bouillon cube. Bring the sauce to a boil, stirring occasionally, making sure the bouillon cube has dissolved. Lower heat and simmer another 10–15 minutes. Taste and season with more salt, if necessary. I find the bouillon cube usually provides plenty of salt.

JILL'S SMART IDEA

After peeling chilis, remember that you do *not* want to do any of the following:

- Feed your baby.
- Put in your contact lenses .
- Use your chili knife or cutting board for anything else without washing both really, *really* well.

seared scallops with beluga lentils, beets and herbs

JEWELS SAYS • Sweet, juicy scallops can be a fantastic change. They are really easy to make but often they are overcooked and can become tough. Use day-boat or dry-pack scallops. I do not recommend using frozen scallops at all, and if you cannot find them fresh, you can use shrimp instead. The sweetness of the beets is offset by the lentils, so be sure to indulge!

SERVES 4–6.

- 6–8 beets, peeled and cut into about 6 pieces each
- a few sprigs of thyme, leaves only
- salt and pepper, to taste
- 12 day-boat scallops (or dry-pack)
- a few glugs of olive oil or 1/4 cup *Jewels' Fantastic Fish Marinade* (page 143)
- 2 cups of *Lentils People Eat* (page 275)
- a handful of flat-leaf parsley, roughly chopped, and/or a few handfuls of arugula, and/or 1/2 bunch of chopped chives

1. Roast the beets with the olive oil, thyme, salt and pepper until tender (about 15–20 minutes) at 400 degrees F.

2. Clean the scallops of the foot and cover them with the olive oil or the marinade and salt and pepper.

3. When the beets are done, remove from oven. Leave the oven on.

4. Heat an oven-safe pan over medium-high heat until hot. Sear the scallops for about 2 minutes on each side.

5. Put the scallops in the oven to finish cooking for about another 2 minutes.

6. Toss the beets, lentils and scallops with the herbs and serve.

JEWELS' SMART IDEA

Save any leftovers and eat cold later.

grilled trevissiano and chicken with matsutake mushrooms

JEWELS SAYS • Trevissiano, a milder cousin to radicchio, is a wonderfully unusual pairing with grilled chicken. Instead of trevissiano, you can swap in radicchio if you prefer its sharper flavor. Like all mushrooms, matsutakes are seasonal, so if they're not available, feel free to use porcinis, which are big and fat and easy to grill.

SERVES 4.

- 4 half chicken breasts, bone in (I like to keep the bottom part of the wing on—in what is often called an "airline cut." Ask your butcher for this cut.)
- salt and pepper
- ³/₄ cup of *Jewels' Grill Marinade* (page 98)
- 8 matsutake mushrooms or fresh porcinis, sliced in half, lengthwise
- 4 large trevissiano or 4 heads radicchio, cut into thirds, lengthwise
- 1 bunch fresh Italian parsley, chopped

1. Preheat a barbecue to medium-high heat.

2. In a shallow pan, season the chicken with salt and pepper by rubbing it into the flesh. Pour ⅓ of the grill marinade over the chicken and rub in with your hands (as always, be *sure* to wash your hands well afterward). Marinate the chicken for 20 minutes to a few hours.

3. Marinate the mushrooms and the trevissiano with the remaining marinade, taking special care not to break the mushrooms. Marinate for 20 minutes to a few hours.

4. Grill the chicken first, turning often. This should take about 15–22 minutes, depending on the thickness of the breasts.

5. When you remove the chicken, turn the heat to high and grill the mushrooms and the trevissiano about 3–4 minutes on each side.

6. Place the trevissiano on the plate, then the chicken, then the mushrooms, and place parsley over the top of the chicken. Enjoy.

"I like straightforward food that is well seasoned and elegantly presented without fuss or deception."

—Jacques Pépin

over, under, on the side

JEWELS SAYS • As a Family Chef I am in constant search of difference. It is my job to keep meals interesting for the families I cook for. One of the best ways to do this is by using new side dishes. There is so much more than just asparagus, spinach or mashed potatoes to accompany your meals. I start the same way I begin most of my cooking: by asking, "What looks fresh?"

Lately the answer is often purslane, a succulent leafy vegetable with roots that's also known as verdulaga. Many people overlook the wild purslane growing in their gardens, but it is indeed edible! It's got a bright citrusy flavor and cooks up a bit like green beans. I like to sauté it with garlic, onions and tomatoes for a yummy side dish. If I throw in a handful of beans, I've got a complete meal.

The other thing about purslane is that it's superrich in vitamins and very healthy, perfect for one of our friends who is wild about her greens.

We admire the simple strategy she follows when watching her weight. She makes sure her meals are full of leafy greens and then she eats most of those greens before she starts in on the main course or a starchy carbohydrate. It's a simple thing, but it can make a great difference to your health! I think that's a great way to look at sides. They're more than an afterthought; they can bring an otherwise simple meal to life.

over, under, on the side

lentils people eat

MAKES ABOUT 4 CUPS.

2 cups lentils (any type), uncooked

4 cups water (approximately)

salt, to taste

a few glugs of delicious extra-virgin olive oil

$^1/_2$ shallot, minced (optional)

1. Pick through the lentils, removing any stones that may have not been removed during packaging.

2. Rinse the lentils with cold water and put in a medium-sized pot. The water should be about 3 times higher than the uncooked lentils since they will double in size.

3. Simmer until tender. For darker lentils like beluga it will take approximately 20–30 minutes and for thinner lentils like crimson or pink it will take approximately 10–15 minutes.

4. When the lentils have finished cooking, add a little salt, to taste. (They will get tough if you add it before they are finished.)

5. You can drain off any excess liquid and toss with olive oil and shallots (if using).

indian-style chickpeas—jill's version

JILL SAYS • I used to think garbanzo beans were something healthy—but not tasty—that people tried to sneak into their salads. But I'm crazy about hummus, so I figured there must be other ways to prepare them. I realized that if you do just a little something with these beans they can be delicious!

SERVES 4–6.

1–2 tablespoons extra-virgin olive oil
$1/2$ medium onion, diced small
1 teaspoon garlic, minced
1 teaspoon ginger, minced
1 serrano or Thai chili, finely chopped
$1/2$ teaspoon ground cumin
$1/2$ teaspoon ground coriander
$1/2$ teaspoon garam masala
a dash of cayenne pepper
$1/2$ teaspoon salt
2 ripe tomatoes, chopped
2 cans garbanzo beans, drained and rinsed
1 small handful of cilantro, roughly chopped

1. Heat a large sauté pan over medium-high heat. When the pan is hot, add the olive oil and sauté the onions, garlic and ginger until soft and translucent, about 3 minutes. Add the serrano chili and sauté another minute or so.

2. Stir in the cumin, coriander, garam masala, cayenne pepper and salt. Add the tomatoes and continue cooking for another 2–3 minutes.

3. Add the garbanzo beans and cook for another 5 minutes or so. Stir in the cilantro and serve.

chickpea salad—jewels' version

JEWELS SAYS • I love to keep a nice cold salad in my refrigerator and snack on it throughout the day. It tastes good with just about anything, including beef, chicken or fish.

SERVES 4–6.

2 cans garbanzo beans, drained and rinsed

1/2 small red onion, diced small

4 ripe Roma tomatoes, seeded and diced small

1 ripe avocado, diced small

2 Persian cucumbers, peeled in stripes and diced small

a handful of flat-leaf parsley, roughly chopped

2–3 glugs extra-virgin olive oil

juice from 1/2 lemon

Mix all of the ingredients together in a bowl.

JEWELS' SMART IDEA

This salad tastes great with warm halloumi cheese.

cavalo nero

JILL SAYS • Whether it's called *cavalo nero*, Tuscan kale, dinosaur kale, lacinato kale or just black kale, this is my favorite green veggie. *Cavalo nero* is much less bitter than other kales and it has great texture and a beautiful deep green color. Like fresh spinach, it shrinks when you cook it up, so use a huge skillet or two pans or do it in batches when making this dish for a lot of people.

SERVES 4–6.

> 2 bunches of *cavalo nero*
> a few glugs of olive oil
> 1 shallot, sliced thin, and/or ½ onion, sliced thin
> 1 clove garlic, smashed and chopped
> salt and pepper, to taste

1. Tear the *cavalo nero* leaves in pieces, leaving out the thick white stem.

2. Rinse the kale well to remove any dirt and debris.

3. Heat a pan over medium heat and sauté in oil the shallot and/or onion and garlic for a moment. Don't brown.

4. Add the *cavalo nero* to the pan and use tongs to help turn the greens in the pan until they wilt and turn bright green, about 5 minutes. You may have to add a tablespoon or so of water to create moisture and keep the greens from browning.

5. Add salt and pepper, to taste.

JILL'S SMART IDEA

Wash the *cavalo nero* when you first bring it home. After rinsing, turn it in a salad spinner to dry and then store in a Ziploc bag with a paper towel inside to absorb any moisture. That way, you'll have fresh *cavalo nero* ready to use throughout the week without taking up too much room in the fridge.

pan-roasted cauliflower

JILL SAYS • This is a wonderful substitute for potatoes. It's a little bit lighter and more flavorful. I really don't think people use cauliflower enough!

SERVES 4–6.

> 2 tablespoons extra-virgin olive oil
>
> 1 head cauliflower, cut into large florets and sliced about ¼" thick
>
> 1 teaspoon garlic, chopped
>
> 2 tablespoons water

1. Heat a large skillet over medium-high heat. When the pan is hot, add the oil and sauté the cauliflower. Let brown a little, then stir, flipping the pieces over to brown on the other side.

2. Add the garlic and sauté for another minute or so. Be careful not to let the garlic burn, which produces a bitter taste.

3. Add a couple tablespoons of water to the pan. Partially cover and cook another 2–3 minutes, until the water evaporates and the cauliflower is soft, but not mushy. The water will create a little steam to finish cooking the cauliflower.

JILL'S SMART IDEA

Instead of using water, add two freshly chopped tomatoes and parsley or cilantro after you have browned the cauliflower. Then cook until the vegetables are soft.

mashed yams

JILL SAYS • I really started loving yams and sweet potatoes after traveling with Simon in Australia, because the Aussies use them in so many things. Personal trainers will often tell you to put them into your diet, because they're so good for you. This is one of my favorite recipes!

SERVES 4–6.

- 4 yams (or sweet potatoes), peeled and cut into large chunks
- 1 teaspoon salt
- 1/4–1/2 cup milk, depending on the size of the yams or sweet potatoes
- 2 tablespoons butter

1. Place the yams in a medium-sized pan. Cover with water and add 1/2 teaspoon salt to the water. Bring to a boil, reduce the heat to medium and cook until the yams are tender and can be pierced easily with a fork.

2. Heat 1/4 cup milk and the butter in a small pan. Drain the yams and return to the pan (not on the flame) along with the milk-and-butter mixture and the remaining salt. Mash until smooth and creamy. Add remaining milk, if necessary.

JILL'S SMART IDEA

Simon likes to cut up scallions and put them in his yams. It's yummy!

prosciutto-wrapped sweet potatoes

JEWELS SAYS • I first saw this recipe in an Italian cookbook and made it for a party of about fifty people, but substituted sweet potatoes for potatoes, because I love the contrast of the sweetness with the saltiness of the prosciutto. A woman who was helping me that night thought I was crazy to actually serve them because I'd never made them before. For some reason, she was actually mad about it—and I couldn't figure out why. Maybe it's not so smart but I do stuff like that! The guests licked their plates that night and asked for more. I mean, who doesn't want prosciutto wrapped around potato? Come on, that's so yummy!

There is often confusion between yams and sweet potatoes. I like to use the white sweet potato for this recipe. If you can't find sweet potatoes, use yams mixed with regular potatoes.

SERVES 6–8.

    4 large sweet potatoes, peeled and cut in to about 1½" pieces
    a few pats of butter
    about a tablespoon of Dijon mustard
    1 egg yolk (optional)
    salt and white pepper, to taste
    3 tablespoons of flour
    8–12 slices of prosciutto de parma, sliced paper-thin
    a few glugs of olive oil
    a few sprigs of parsley, roughly chopped

1. Put the sweet potato pieces in a pot and cover with cold water and a dash of salt. Cook the sweet potatoes until tender and drain any excess water.

2. In a mixer or food processor, mix the cooked sweet potatoes with butter, Dijon mustard and egg yolk, if using. Season with salt and white pepper, to taste. Let potatoes cool slightly before wrapping in prosciutto.

3. Turn the oven on to 375 degrees F.

4. Lay a thin strip of the prosciutto, lengthwise, on a piece of parchment paper. Layer another next to it, overlapping slightly along the long side, and continue until you have used about 4–6 pieces of prosciutto.

5. Generously spoon the mashed sweet potato horizontally across the bottom third of the proscuitto strips (the end closest to you). You should use about half the mixture when you do this.

6. Starting with the end nearest you and using the parchment paper to help you shape and hold the roll, roll up the prosciutto, rolling away from you. Shape the roll and pack the ends as you go to evenly distribute the potato mixture. Take care not to let the parchment get stuck inside the roll.

7. At this point, the prosciutto and sweet potato roll should be held together with the parchment wrapped around it.

8. Using a very sharp knife, cut 4–6 even slices while still keeping the paper wrapped around the roll. Take care not to put any pressure on the roll or you will squeeze out the sweet potatoes.

9. Gently unwrap the parchment from each piece of the sliced roll and dust a little flour on all the ends. Set aside.

10. Repeat steps 4–9 with the remaining prosciutto and sweet potato.

11. Heat a pan over medium heat until warm. Add a glug of oil and panfry both ends of each slice until browned, adding extra oil as necessary. Place on baking sheet.

12. When all pieces are fried, place the baking sheet in the oven and bake for 10 minutes.

13. Sprinkle with parsley and serve.

JILL'S SMART IDEA

If you plan to make this for a dinner party, of course, I suggest you make it beforehand!

red cabbage coleslaw, 3 ways

JILL SAYS • Coleslaw can be a great accompaniment to many dishes. Change the dressing on your slaw and you completely change its character and flavor. It's a simple and very inexpensive side that can feed a lot of people.

SERVES 6–8.
- 1 head red cabbage, cored and sliced thinly with knife or mandolin
- 1 Maui or Vidalia onion, cut in half and sliced super-thin

Use one of the dressings below. Let the cabbage marinate in its dressing for about 15 minutes before serving.

dressing 1

MAKES ABOUT 1 CUP.
- 1/4 cup red wine vinegar
- 1/4 teaspoon minced garlic
- 1/2 teaspoon salt
- 2 teaspoons sugar
- 3/4 cup extra-virgin olive oil

Put all of the ingredients in a jar and shake.

dressing 2

MAKES ABOUT 1 1/2 CUPS.
- 3 tablespoons seasoned rice wine vinegar
- 1 tablespoon lime juice
- 1/2 teaspoon salt
- 1 tablespoon honey
- 1/2 teaspoon ginger, minced
- 1/4 teaspoon garlic, minced
- 1 tablespoon soy sauce
- 2 tablespoons sesame oil
- 1/2 cup peanut oil
- 1/4 cup cashews or peanuts, finely chopped (in food processor)

Put all of the ingredients in a jar and shake.

dressing 3

MAKES 1¾ CUPS.

- 3 tablespoons lemon juice
- ¼ cup mayonnaise
- ¾ cup olive oil
- 2 tablespoons prepared horseradish
- 2 teaspoons sugar
- salt and pepper, to taste

Put all of the ingredients in a jar and shake.

JILL'S SMART IDEA

I like to use any leftovers from this recipe on a sandwich the next day. It's also good with leftover grilled fish wrapped in a whole-wheat tortilla.

"It's bizarre that the produce manager is more important to my children's health than the pediatrician."

—Meryl Streep

new and improved succotash

JILL SAYS • In my experience, not everyone loves lima beans, but most people, even kids, do like edamame. This succotash is a fresh twist, one the whole family will love. Get a helper of any age to shuck the corn and, if you can't find edamame beans shelled, have your helper shell those, too.

SERVES 4–6.
- 1 tablespoon extra-virgin olive oil
- 1 tablespoon butter
- 1 medium onion, diced into small pieces, or 2 small shallots, thinly sliced
- $1/2$ teaspoon garlic, minced
- 6 ears of corn, husked and kernels sliced off
- $1^1/2$ cups edamame beans, thawed (can be purchased in the frozen food section of the market)
- $1/2$ teaspoon salt

1. Heat a large skillet on the stove over medium-high heat. When the pan is hot, add the olive oil and butter and sauté the onions until very soft and translucent, about 5 minutes. Add the garlic and sauté another 2 minutes.

2. Add corn kernels and continue to sauté and stir for another 3 minutes or so, until the corn becomes translucent. Add the edamame and salt. Cook until the edamame is warm. The corn should still be crispy. Add $1/2$ teaspoon salt or to taste.

JILL'S SMART IDEA

Keep an eye on any kids who help you shell the edamame, because they usually eat half of them before finishing the job!

veggie spaghetti

JEWELS SAYS • My mom gave me this idea when I wanted to serve spaghetti to a low-carb group. They were so excited that they could actually have spaghetti sauce! They loved it. The vegetables are cut on a Japanese mandolin, which should be handled by adults only and with extra care, *so do not use it if you are in a rush.* It comes with a plastic guard, which should always be used when you are operating the mandolin. When cutting something hard like sweet potatoes or carrots, don't force the blade if it is not moving. Turn the vegetable, the center of which tends to be hard, a quarter inch and try again. This dish is great with our *Quick Meat Sauce* (page 224), fresh herbs and Parmesan, or any sauce you would put on pasta.

SERVES 4–6.

  6 carrots, peeled

  4 green zucchini

  4 yellow zucchini or yellow crookneck squash

  a glug of olive oil

  6 leaves opal basil or green basil, thinly sliced (optional)

  salt and pepper, to taste

1. Set a mandolin to the julienne setting and slice the carrots and zucchini. If you don't have a mandolin, you can julienne the veggies with a sharp knife, slicing as thin as possible.

2. Heat a pan large enough to accommodate all the veggies over medium heat. After a minute, add a glug of olive oil.

3. Sauté the veggies until just barely softened, about a minute or two. Sprinkle with salt and pepper to taste and top with basil (if using).

JEWELS' SMART IDEA

When you've finished using your mandolin, put the guard over the blade, wrap it in Saran Wrap two or three times and store it upside down so that there is no way to cut yourself accidentally when you stick your hand in the drawer. Wrap the extra blades in Saran Wrap for safekeeping, too. The mandolin is a great tool if you're careful. You can buy one at almost any Asian market and most high-quality cooking supply stores (see *Resources*).

quinoa with crunchy veggies and fresh herbs

JEWELS SAYS • A protein and a carbohydrate, quinoa is the perfect food. This is a wonderfully simple way to prepare it, added to a salad.

the quinoa

1 cup quinoa

2 cups cold water

$1/2$ teaspoon salt

1. Put the quinoa in a fine sieve and rinse with cold running water to remove the saponin, a glycoside that tends to froth and that can be a little bitter.

2. Put the rinsed quinoa in a pot and add water and salt.

3. Cook until tender and all the "kernels" have burst, about 20 minutes. Remove from heat and leave covered, about 5 minutes.

4. Drain any excess water and season with salt and extra-virgin olive oil.

the salad

SERVES 4–6.

2 celery stalks, chopped small

3–4 Persian cucumbers, chopped small

$1/2$ bulb fennel, chopped small

1 small shallot, chopped fine

$1/2$ bunch chives, chopped

1 bunch parsley, chopped

1 handful Marcona almonds

1 big handful of Granglona pecorino cheese

a few drizzles of extra-virgin olive oil

a few drizzles of sherry wine vinegar

salt and pepper, for seasoning

Toss the ingredients together to make a delicious salad, add quinoa—and enjoy!

jill's favorite calibasita

JILL SAYS • Like most kids, corn has been one of my favorite vegetables ever since I was little. This recipe is something our nana used to make all the time. I think it may have been her way of getting me to eat something other than just corn—and it worked. She called it calibasita, which in Spanish literally means "little squash." It's really delicious and I highly recommend trying this as a side dish for kids. It's a great way of getting them to eat zucchini—which isn't a favorite for most kids!

SERVES 4–6.

- 4 small green zucchini, diced into $1/2$" pieces
- 2 teaspoons kosher salt
- 2 tablespoons olive oil
- 1 medium onion, diced
- 1 small garlic clove, minced (or $1/4$ teaspoon garlic powder)
- 4 ears fresh corn, husked and kernels sliced off
- 2 Roma tomatoes, seeded and diced into $1/2$" pieces
- $1/2$ cup grated mozzarella cheese (optional)

1. Place the diced zucchini in a colander and toss with salt. Place the colander over a bowl and let sit, 20–30 minutes. The salt will bring out the liquid from the zucchini.

2. Remove the zucchini and place on a kitchen towel. Gently pat the zucchini dry to remove any additional moisture. This step is optional, but in my opinion worth the extra time for two reasons: Drying zucchini prior to sautéing it keeps it from becoming watery, and I think this step removes the zucchini's occasional bitterness.

3. In a medium-sized sauté pan, heat the olive oil over medium-high heat. Add the onions and garlic; when you do, the oil should sizzle. Sauté 3–5 minutes, stirring occasionally, until the onions are soft and translucent. Do not brown.

4. Add the zucchini and corn kernels and sauté another 10 minutes, stirring occasionally. You may need to lower the heat to medium to prevent the vegetables from browning.

5. Add the diced tomato and sauté another 2–3 minutes. Stir in cheese, if desired.

JILL'S SMART IDEA

I love adding leftover calibasita to scrambled eggs in the morning for a breakfast burrito. Add a dash of hot sauce, roll it up and hit the road!

a few final thoughts

WE'D NEVER CLAIM that making fresh, delicious food every day is *easy*. But, while we don't think it's hard either, we do understand that it requires an investment of time, money, thoughtfulness and a little creativity.

We also believe this investment couldn't be more worth it—one on which you will see a manyfold return. Taking up the apron of the Family Chef is one of the best gifts you can give to yourself and to your family. As Jamie Oliver says, "What we eat affects everything: our mood, behavior, health, growth, even our ability to concentrate." To that, we'd add that what and how we eat affects our health as a family and our relations with the people we love most. We believe families who enjoy wonderful meals together stay together, too.

As the Family Chef who gets everybody chopping and stirring, you have the power to improve the health and well-being of both yourself and your family members—while having a blast at the same time!

We want to support you on your adventures as a Family Chef! So, e-mail us at jandj@JewelsandJill.com and let us know how it's going!

Bon appétit!
Jewels and Jill

resources

IF YOU LIVE in a city as we do, you'll probably find most of the more exotic ingredients and equipment we use in your local stores, ethnic markets and farmers' markets. If you are fortunate enough to live near ethnic communities, we encourage you to explore the shops there; you're sure to find what you need at far better prices. As our culture becomes more worldly, you may also be surprised to find that large national grocery store chains now carry many of these items. For anything you cannot find, here are some reliable online sources we suggest you try.

achiote paste
brand we prefer: la perla del mayab

Kalustyan's
http://www.kalustyans.com
123 Lexington Avenue
New York, NY 10016
(800) 352-3451

Gourmetsleuth
http://www.gourmetsleuth.com
P.O. Box 508
Los Gatos, CA 95031
(408) 354-8281

MexGrocer.com
http://www.mexgrocer.com
4060 Morena Boulevard, Suite C
San Diego, CA 92117
(877) 463-9476

air-chilled chicken
MBA Poultry
www.smartchicken.com
13151 Dovers Street
P.O. Box 470
Waverly, NE 68462
(402) 786-1000

ancho chile powder
Kalustyan's
http://www.kalustyans.com
123 Lexington Avenue
New York, NY 10016
(800) 352-3451

Purcell Mountain Farms
http://www.purcellmountainfarms.com
393 Firehouse Road
Moyie Springs, ID 83845
(208) 267-0627

Gourmetsleuth
http://www.gourmetsleuth.com
P.O. Box 508
Los Gatos, CA 95031
(408) 354–8281

bonito flakes
Mitsuwa Marketplace
https://shop.mitsuwa.com
Visit Web site to find a store near you or
shop online.

Asian Food Grocer
http://www.asianfoodgrocer.com
131 West Harris Avenue
South San Francisco, CA 94080
(888) 482–2742

brown kalijira rice
brand we prefer: lotus foods

Kalustyan's
http://www.kalustyans.com
123 Lexington Avenue
New York, NY 10016
(212) 685–3451

World Pantry
http://www.worldpantry.com
Lotus Foods, Inc.
921 Richmond Street
El Cerrito, CA 94530
(510) 525–3137

brown rice vinegar
Spectrum Organics
http://www.spectrumorganics.com
Spectrum Organic Products, LLC
1105 Industrial Avenue
Petaluma, CA 94952

Eden Foods
http://www.edenfoods.com
Eden Foods, Inc.
701 Tecumseh Road
Clinton, MI 49236
(888) 424–3336

cedar plank
Williams-Sonoma
http://www.williams-sonoma.com
Visit Web site to find a store near you or
shop online.

Sur La Table
http://www.surlatable.com
Visit Web site to find a store near you or
shop online.

North Woods Smoke of Minnesota
http://www.northwoodssmokeofmn.com
9828 170th Avenue
Royalton, MN 56373
(320) 584–5025

champagne vinegar
igourmet.com
http://www.igourmet.com
508 Delaware Avenue
West Pittston, PA 18643
(877) 446–8763

Sparrow Lane
http://www.sparrowlane.com
P.O. Box 642
Keyes, CA 95328
(866) 515–2477

coconut vinegar
brand we prefer: silver swan

Pinoy Grocery
http://store.pinoygrocery.com
811 South Mason Road
Suite 116
Katy, TX 77450
(281) 829-9798

Borcay Filipino Market
http://www.boracayfilipinomarket.com
14425 7th Street
Victorville, CA 92392
(760) 955-9128

***cotija* cheese**
brand we prefer: cacique

Cacique
http://www.caciqueusa.com
(800) 521-6987
Call to find a distribution store in your area.

Igourmet
http://www.igourmet.com
(877) 446-8763

Cheese Supply
https://www.cheesesupply.com
P.O. Box 31125
Bellingham, WA 98228
(866) 205-6376

fideo noodles (or misko noodles or angel hair nests)
La Tienda
http://www.tienda.com
3601 La Grange Parkway
Toano, VA 23168
(800) 710-4304

Marky's
http://www.markys.com
687 Northeast 79th Street
Miami, FL 33138
(800) 522-8427

Greekshops.com (for misko noodles)
http://www.greekshops.com
2665 30th Street, Suite 214
Santa Monica, CA 90405
(310) 581-5059

forbidden rice (chinese black rice)
Kalustyan's
http://www.kalustyans.com
123 Lexington Avenue
New York, NY 10016
(212) 685-3451

Purcell Mountain Farms
http://www.purcellmountainfarms.com
393 Firehouse Road
Moyie Springs, ID 83845
(208) 267-0627

french lentils (green lentils, *lentils de puy*)
Kalustyan's
http://www.kalustyans.com
123 Lexington Avenue
New York, NY 10016
(212) 685-3451

Purcell Mountain Farms
http://www.purcellmountainfarms.com
393 Firehouse Road
Moyie Springs, ID 83845
(208) 267–0627

ChefShop.com
http://gourmet.chefshop.com
P.O. Box 3488
Seattle, WA 98114
(800) 596–0885

frigoverre
Chefs
http://www.chefscatalog.com
5070 Centennial Boulevard
Colorado Springs, CO 80919
(800) 338–3232

furikake
Mitsuwa Marketplace
https://shop.mitsuwa.com
Visit Web site to find a store near you or shop online.

Asian Food Grocer
http://www.asianfoodgrocer.com
131 West Harris Avenue
South San Francisco, CA 94080
(888) 482–2742

garam masala
Kalustyan's
http://www.kalustyans.com
123 Lexington Avenue
New York, NY 10016
(212) 685–3451

The Spice House
http://www.thespicehouse.com
(847) 328–3711
Visit Web site for a store near you or shop online.

gyoza skins
Mitsuwa Marketplace
https://shop.mitsuwa.com
Visit Web site to find a store near you or shop online.

halloumi cheese
brand we prefer: cypriot

Igourmet
http://www.igourmet.com
(877) 446–8763

Cheese Supply
https://www.cheesesupply.com
P.O. Box 31125
Bellingham, WA 98228
(866) 205–6376

hoison sauce
Chinese FoodsDIY
http://www.chinesefooddiy.com

Asian Food Grocer
http://www.asianfoodgrocer.com
131 West Harris Avenue
South San Francisco, CA 94080
(888) 482–2742

japanese bento boxes

Mrs. Lin's Kitchen
http://www.mrslinskitchen.com
5627 Stoneridge Drive #306
Pleasanton, CA 94588
(925) 251-0158

Asian Art Mall
http://www.asianartmall.com
4 Nashua Court, Bay 11
Baltimore, MD 21221
(888) 846-7436

kaffir lime leaves

Importfood.com
http://importfood.com
P.O. Box 2054
Issaquah, WA 98027
(888) 618-8424

Savory Spice Shop
http://www.savoryspiceshop.com
1537 Platte Street
Denver, CO 80202
(303) 477-3322

kombu

Asian Food Grocer
http://www.asianfoodgrocer.com
131 West Harris Avenue
South San Francisco, CA 94080
(888) 482-2742

kurobuta pork

Snake River Farms
www.snakeriverfarms.com
555 Shoreline Drive, 3rd Floor
Boise, ID 83702

maitake mushrooms

Kalustyan's
http://www.kalustyans.com
123 Lexington Avenue
New York, NY 10016
(212) 685-3451

MingsPantry.com
http://www.mingspantry.com
c/o Famous Foods Inc.
376 Nash Road
New Bedford, MA 02746
(866) 646-4266

Oregon Mushroom
http://oregonmushrooms.rtrk.com
11489 Red Wing Loop
P.O. Box 1025
Keno, OR 97627
(877) 889-6015

mandolin (japanese/asian)

Sur La Table
http://www.surlatable.com
*Visit Web site to find a store near you or
shop online.*

Cooking.com
http://www.cooking.com
2850 Ocean Park Boulevard, Suite 310
Santa Monica, CA 90405
(800) 663-8810

matsutake mushrooms

Oregon Mushroom
http://oregonmushrooms.rtrk.com
11489 Red Wing Loop
P.O. Box 1025
Keno, OR 97627
(877) 889-6015

Pacific Rim Mushrooms
http://www.pacrimmushrooms.com
c/o Brenton King
403–1435 Nelson Street
Vancouver, BC
V6G 2Z3, Canada
(604) 568–6033

microplaner

Williams-Sonoma
http://www.williams-sonoma.com
Visit Web site to find a store near you or shop online.

Sur La Table
http://www.surlatable.com
Visit Web site to find a store near you or shop online.

Chef's Resource
http://www.chefsresource.com
22732-B Granite Way
Laguna Hills, CA 92653
(949) 581–3797

miso (white, sakiro, shiro)

Earthy Delights
http://www.earthy.com
1161 E. Clark Road, Suite 260
DeWitt, MI 48820
(800) 367–4709

Asian Food Grocer
http://www.asianfoodgrocer.com
131 West Harris Avenue
South San Francisco, CA 94080
(888) 482–2742

morel mushrooms

Kalustyan's
http://www.kalustyans.com
123 Lexington Avenue
New York, NY 10016
(212) 685–3451

Marky's
http://www.markys.com
687 Northeast 79th Street
Miami, FL 33138
(800) 522–8427

Oregon Mushroom
http://oregonmushrooms.rtrk.com
11489 Red Wing Loop
P.O. Box 1025
Keno, OR 97627
(877) 889–6015

nori

Mitsuwa Marketplace
https://shop.mitsuwa.com
Visit Web site to find a store near you or shop online.

Kalustyan's
http://www.kalustyans.com
123 Lexington Avenue
New York, NY 10016
(212) 685–3451

Asian Food Grocer
http://www.asianfoodgrocer.com
131 West Harris Avenue
South San Francisco, CA 94080
(888) 482–2742

olive salt

Surfas
https://www.surfasonline.com
3975 Landmark Street
Culver City, CA 90232
(866) 799-4770

paella pans

La Tienda
http://www.tienda.com
3601 La Grange Parkway
Toano, VA 23168
(800) 710-4304

Williams-Sonoma
http://www.williams-sonoma.com
*Visit Web site to find a store near you or
shop online.*

Sur La Table
http://www.surlatable.com
*Visit Web site to find a store near you or
shop online.*

paul prudhomme's
blackened redfish magic

Chef Paul
http://shop.chefpaul.com
Magic Seasoning Blends
824 Distributors Row
Harahan, LA 70123
(800) 457-2857

pecorino romano cheese

we prefer: il granglona

The Cheese Store of Beverly Hills
http://www.cheesestorebh.com
419 North Beverly Drive
Beverly Hills, CA 90210
(800) 547-1515

Murray's Cheese
www.murrayscheese.com
254 Bleecker St.
New York, NY 10014
(888) 692-4339

Artisanal Cheese
http://www.artisanalcheese.com
(877) 797-1200

pomegranate concentrate

Wellness Grocer
http://www.wellnessgrocer.com
(888) 272-8775

Iherb.com
http://www.iherb.com
5012 4th Street
Irwindale, CA 91706
(866) 328-1171

reuseable bags

Reusablebags.com
http://www.reusablebags.com
116 W. Illinois Street, Suite 6E
Chicago, IL 60654
(773) 912-1562

san marzano tomatoes
La Cucina Rustica LLC
http://www.cybercucina.com
1800 West Hawthorne Lane, Suite 203
West Chicago, IL 60185
(800) 796–0116

Fine products International
http://www.fineproductsinternational.com
P.O. Box 1361
Voorhees, NJ 08043

shelton's organic chicken stock
Shelton's Poultry, Inc.
http://www.sheltons.com
204 North Loranne
Pomona, CA 91767
(800) 541–1833

sherry vinegar
Zingerman's Delicatessan
http://www.zingermans.com
620 Phoenix Drive
Ann Arbor, MI 48108
(888) 636–8162

Igourmet
http://www.igourmet.com
(877) 446–8763

shitake mushrooms
Kalustyan's
http://www.kalustyans.com
123 Lexington Avenue
New York, NY 10016
(212) 685–3451

Marky's
http://www.markys.com
687 Northeast 79th Street
Miami, FL 33138
(800) 522–8427

Oregon Mushroom
http://oregonmushrooms.rtrk.com
11489 Red Wing Loop
P.O. Box 1025
Keno, OR 97627
(877) 889–6015

silpat
Williams-Sonoma
http://www.williams-sonoma.com
Visit Web site to find a store near you or shop online.

Sur La Table
http://www.surlatable.com
Visit Web site to find a store near you or shop online.

Cooking.com
http://www.cooking.com
2850 Ocean Park Boulevard, Suite 310
Santa Monica, CA 90405
(800) 663–8810

spaghettini
Cube Marketplace
http://www.cubemarketplace.com
615 North La Brea Avenue
Los Angeles, CA 90036
(888) 23-PASTA

ChefShop
http://gourmet.chefshop.com
P.O. Box 3488
Seattle, WA 98114
(800) 596-0885

sriracha (hot chili sauce)
Cosmic Chile
http://www.cosmicchile.com
1612 Gold Avenue
Bozeman, MT 59715
(800) 955-9724

Grocery Thai
http://grocerythai.com
10929 Vanowen Street, Suite 143
North Hollywood, CA 91605
(818) 469-9407

tagine
Williams-Sonoma
http://www.williams-sonoma.com
Visit Web site to find a store near you or shop online.

Sur La Table
http://www.surlatable.com
Visit Web site to find a store near you or shop online.

Tagines by Berber Trading Company
http://www.tagines.com
5-27 Northeast 39th Street
Miami, FL 33137
(305) 572-0118

tagliolini
brand we prefer: spinosi

Cube Marketplace
http://www.cubemarketplace.com
615 North La Brea Avenue
Los Angeles, CA 90036
(888) 23-PASTA

Olio E Olive Store
http://www.olioeolivestore.com
6068 Center Drive, 6th Floor
Los Angeles, CA 90045
(310) 242-5955

tahini
Kalustyan's
http://www.kalustyans.com
123 Lexington Avenue
New York, NY 10016
(800) 352-3451

The Spice House
http://www.thespicehouse.com
(847) 328-3711
Visit Web site for a store near you or shop online.

Nuts Online
http://www.nutsonline.com
1201 East Linden Avenue
Linden, NJ 07036
(800) 558-6887

tapatío hot sauce
Tapatío
http://www.tapatiohotsauce.com
(323) 587-8933

MexGrocer.com
http://www.mexgrocer.com
4060 Morena Boulevard, Suite C
San Diego, CA 92117
(877) 463–9476

truffle oil
Marky's
http://www.markys.com
687 Northeast 79th Street
Miami, FL 33138
(800) 522–8427

Igourmet
http://www.igourmet.com
(877) 446–8763

Oregon Mushroom
http://oregonmushrooms.rtrk.com
11489 Red Wing Loop
P.O. Box 1025
Keno, OR 97627
(877) 889–6015

truffle salt
The Spice House
http://www.thespicehouse.com
(847) 328–3711
*Visit Web site for a store near you or shop
online.*

The Savory Pantry
http://www.savorypantry.com
214 Central Avenue
Hot Springs National Park, AR 71901
(877) 426–4887

La Cucina Rustica LLC
http://www.cybercucina.com
1800 West Hawthorne Lane, Suite 203
West Chicago, IL 60185
(800) 796–0116

wasabi
The Spice House
http://www.thespicehouse.com
(847) 328–3711
*Visit Web site for a store near you or shop
online.*

Mitsuwa Marketplace
https://shop.mitsuwa.com
*Visit Web site to find a store near you or
shop online.*

jewels' favorite books

The Apprentice: My Life in the Kitchen by Jacques Pépin (Houghton Mifflin, May 7, 2004)

The Complete Meat Cookbook by Bruce Aidells and Denis Kelly (Houghton Mifflin; 1st edition, September 25, 2001)

Cooking by James Peterson (Ten Speed Press, October 2007)

Cracking the Coconut: Classic Thai Home Cooking by Su-Mei Yu (William Morrow Cookbooks; 1st edition, July 3, 2000)

Desserts by the Yard: From Brooklyn to Beverly Hills: Recipes from the Sweetest Life Ever by Sherry Yard (Houghton Mifflin; 1st edition, November 1, 2007)

The French Laundry Cookbook by Thomas Keller (Artisan; 2nd edition, November 1, 1999)

I Am Almost Always Hungry: Seasonal Menus and Memorable Recipes by Lora Zarubin (Harry N. Abrams, October 1, 2003)

Morimoto: The New Art of Japanese Cooking by Masaharu Morimoto (DK Publishing, August 20, 2007)

The Perfectionist: Life and Death in Haute Cuisine by Rudolph Chelminski (Gotham, May 18, 2006)

Raw Food Real World by Mathew Kenney and Sarma Melngailis (William Morrow Cookbooks; 1st edition, July 5, 2005)

A Return to Cooking by Eric Ripert and Michael Ruhlman (Artisan, November 4, 2002)

Tropical Asian Cooking: Exotic Flavors from Equatorial Asia by Wendy Hutton and Nobuyuki Matsuhisa (Periplus Editions, May 15, 2002)

jill's favorite books

Classic Indian Cooking by Julie Sahni (William Morrow Cookbooks; 1st edition, October 1, 1980)

Italian Easy London River Café by Rose Gray and Ruth Rogers (Clarkson Potter, June 15, 2004)

Italian Two Easy London River Café by Rose Gray and Ruth Rogers (Clarkson Potter, June 13, 2006)

Jamie's Dinners: The Essential Family Cookbook by Jamie Oliver (Hyperion, November 3, 2004)

Jamie's Kitchen by Jamie Oliver (Hyperion; 1st edition, October 8, 2003)

Lidia's Family Table: More Than 200 Fabulous Recipes to Enjoy Every Day—With Wonderful Ideas for Variations and Improvisations by Lidia Matticchio Bastianich (Knopf, November 23, 2004)

Mesa Mexicana by Mary Sue Milliken and Susan Feniger (William Morrow Cookbooks; 1st edition, September 23, 1994)

Sunday Suppers at Lucques: Seasonal Recipes from Market to Table by Suzanne Goin
and Teri Gelber (Knopf, November 8, 2005)

Tyler's Ultimate: Brilliant, Simple Food to Make Anytime by Tyler Florence (Clarkson
Potter, September 26, 2006)

The Way to Cook by Julia Child (Knopf, September 28, 1993)

Wolfgang Puck Makes It Easy: Delicious Recipes for Your Home Kitchen by Wolfgang
Puck (Thomas Nelson, August 30, 2008)

our favorite movies

Babette's Feast

Big Night

Chocolat

Dinner Rush

Last Holiday

Like Water for Chocolate

Mostly Martha (original German)

No Reservations (American remake)

Ratatouille

Soul Food

Tortilla Soup

Woman on Top

many thank-yous!

WE ARE GRATEFUL to so many people, none more so than our families.

Jewels: To Kiko—my "Big"—you have given "me anything I want," and so much more. I am, truly, the luckiest girl in the world. You are my rock. Your love and devotion to our family makes me so proud to be your wife. And to my sweet son, Austin, you are my greatest gift.

Jill: Thank you, Simon, for having faith in me, being patient and encouraging me, and for the way you love me and Charlie. I love you, babe. To my little Charlie, you inspire me every day to be the best person I can be.

To our mom and dad, thank you for teaching us to dream big and for making us believe we could do anything! Mom, you will always be the most amazing Family Chef! And, Daddy, you are always perfect in our eyes.

To our brother, JP, also known as "El Rey," we're so happy to be your favorite sisters. Thank you for fighting your battle with so much strength and grace. You are a hero and an inspiration to us both!

To Lynn, we're so grateful to you for traveling halfway around the world to support us as we finished this book. Charlie loves you—and so do we!

To Mandy, our "sistercousin," for your never-ending support and belief in us—and for all the laugh therapy!

Jill: To Karrie, my best friend and kindred spirit, my cooking partner and fellow "Fanilow." You are, indeed, the best friend anyone could ever have.

Jewels: To Jen, my boss lady and friend. Oh, Mamma! You are one of a kind. You have changed my life. You have a completely open heart and always, always, *always* make me feel so appreciated. I admire your incredible generosity of spirit and the deep appreciation you bring to all you have and do. Simply saying thank you just isn't enough to communicate the gratitude Jill and I have for your unbelievable love and support. I can't believe the amazing family you have created around you—and given to us! I am eternally grateful.

To my work family, Carolyn, West and Phill, I can't believe how much you put up with me. I love you all so much.

To our dear friend Guisella, you have played a huge part in all our Family Kitchens—and saved us so many times! We've been through a lot together, lady.

Jill: To Garth and Maggie, for believing in me and giving me the extraordinary opportunity to work in your kitchen in Fiji.

To wonderful Kristin Haan, who helped us learn to "write ourselves." We cannot tell you how much we appreciate your words of wisdom, your valuable time and talent, and your kind heart.

To our dearest Louise, you are an amazing chef and an even better friend! Can you believe how much food we eat together!

Jill: To Alice and Jordan for being amazingly supportive friends.

Jewels: To Maria and family. Being in your home truly taught me how to be a Family Chef. Maria, you are a shining example to me of how to balance your devotion to family, career and your highest ideals. You made me see and believe that it can be done. You are an amazing woman.

Jill: To my work family, thank you for making me feel a part of your family always, for all the amazing opportunities you've shared with me over the years and for your warmth and friendship.

To Jewels' first regular clients, Gayla and Mike Hope, for going above and beyond to promote the "sister chefs." You always make us feel like we are something special!

To JT and Miss Kelly, thank you for the most amazing ride of our lives, your incredible generosity and for challenging us to be the best chefs we could be. We love you.

To the Perlmans! For the food, the wine and for giving Jewels her own menorah. Thank you for the Hawaii trip and your unwavering support when we lost our nana. You are completely amazing. *Muchas gracias, Angelina y Dulce, por su trabajo duro.*

To Melinda Goodman and family, for all the fun we've had in your Family Kitchen. We love you. Aloha.

Jewels: To Julie and Kenny Moelis, what a beautiful family to cook for! Thank you for always making me feel welcome.

To Jamie Oliver, you are a true inspiration to us. Thank you for being so generous with your time and sharing so much of your expertise.

To Wolfgang Puck, our admiration for your hard work and amazing talent is surpassed only by our gratitude. Jewels: Thank you for always finding something nice to say about me. Your beautiful kitchen family—the incredible Sherri, Thomas, Lee, Ari, Mishel, Tracy and Patti—always make me feel so welcome. And to Pam Brunson, for reminding the boss I existed and putting me on the job!

Jewels: To Susan Edelstein, for saying I made perfectly balanced crab cakes and making me believe I had talent.

To Carl Bendix, thank you for taking a chance and having faith in us when we were just babies. You actually thought Jewels' crazy ideas were good ones!

To Dave Rubel, for answering every question we asked you about food and showing us your secrets.

To Rambo, Joel, Armando and Nancy, you are an amazing crew to work with.

To Inna Poncher, thank you for everything. Jewels: Thank you for taking me on the trip that changed my life!

To Randy, Gary, Steve and Emily (I miss you!)—The Originals—for giving me a chance to be a Family Chef with you before I could even grill.

To Coach Morgan, who brought us oranges. Jewels: Thank you for knowing I was different and teaching me how to embrace it.

Jewels: To Ozzie Sosa, who showed me how to look for a job and took me on my very first job interview.

To Tim Noyes, the first person to introduce me to the amazing worlds of sushi, Korean BBQ, and Thai and Indian foods—and so much more. You are a very important part of my journey, in so many ways.

To Marilee and Spencer, thank you for your talent and magic.

An exceptional crew of talented people helped us pull this book together.

To our photographer, Petrina Tinslay, you are *amazing*! From the very first Polaroid, we knew we'd never be able to thank you enough for bringing our food to life. Thank you for the incredible detailed work and for sharing your gift with us. We are eternally grateful for your valuable guidance and kindness.

To Jess, for your hard work and encouragement—and for keeping us laughing.

To our friend and coauthor, Ann Marsh, thank you for bringing us back from the dead! Thank you for the long days and the late nights. You really "get us." We are so grateful for you and your amazing talent.

To Ray Garcia at Celebra, who believes in the power of the Family Chef and did so right from the beginning. *Muchas gracias por todo.*

To Kim Suarez, thank you for listening, caring and always being so responsive.

To our agent, Mel Berger. We are two lucky girls having you look out for us!

To our editor, Tracy Bernstein, thank you for your insightful guidance and meticulous work.

To our assistant, Ami, thank you for the late nights and long days combing through recipes and checking every detail. We love your fantastic attitude!

To Max, our very own Tech God and foodie, all in one.

And to Tess, for the big save.

index